STUDIES IN MODERN EUROPEAN
LITERATURE AND THOUGHT

General Editors:

ERICH HELLER
Professor of German
at Northwestern University

ANTHONY THORLBY
Lecturer in German
at the University of Sussex

ALBERT CAMUS

ALSO PUBLISHED IN THIS SERIES:

FURTHER TITLES ARE IN PREPARATION

ALBERT CAMUS

BY

NATHAN A. SCOTT

Associate Professor of Theology and Literature
The Divinity School
The University of Chicago

NEW YORK
HILLARY HOUSE PUBLISHERS LTD
1962

First published in the U.S.A. by
HILLARY HOUSE PUBLISHERS LTD
New York
1962

Printed in Great Britain
by Richard Clay and Company, Ltd,
Bungay, Suffolk

TO MY SON NATHAN

ACKNOWLEDGMENTS

Portions of this essay first appeared in the form of an article ("The Modest Optimism of Albert Camus") in the December 1959 issue of *The Christian Scholar* (Vol. XLII, No. 4), and I am indebted to the Editor, Professor J. Edward Dirks of Yale University, for permitting me to incorporate them into this book.

Since Camus' career in the English-speaking world has been so well served by Stuart Gilbert, Justin O'Brien, and Anthony Bower, I have chosen, wherever possible, to draw my quotations from their translations; though I have, of course, based my analysis of the *œuvre* on the reading of the French texts. For permission to use these quotations I am indebted to the courtesy of Alfred A. Knopf, Inc. Footnotes are not provided for the quotations from Camus, since it was thought that they would needlessly augment the size and complication of the text.

". . . une certaine continuité dans le désespoir peut engendrer la joie. . . ."

—Albert Camus

ALBERT CAMUS

I

There is perhaps no other European writer of our
period who has exerted so great a pressure on the
imagination and conscience of his generation as has
Albert Camus, whose life, at the age of forty-six,
abruptly ended in an automobile accident in the
south of France on 4 January 1960. And his role
in contemporary cultural life is one that puts us in
mind of how unstable have been the lines of
demarcation in our time between literature and
philosophy. This is undoubtedly in part a result
of the fact that the philosophy of the academies has
often been so intimidated by science that it has
consented to be deprived of first one and then
another of its fields of inquiry, so that, at the last,
there is little else left for it to do but to practise the
disciplines of logical and linguistic analysis. And
thus, for instruction in the unique facts and experiences of human personality, the men of our age
have turned to poets and novelists or to thinkers
like Heidegger and Jaspers and Marcel, who have
been converting philosophy itself into a kind of
metaphysical poetry or drama. But, however we
choose to account for this tendency today of literary
and philosophical categories to coalesce, it must be
granted that in a very deep and integral sense the
great literature of our age has been by way of
becoming "an instrument of metaphysical consciousness."[1] The art of such writers, for example,

[1] Gaëtan Picon, *André Malraux* (Paris: Gallimard, 1945),
p. 64.

as Pirandello and Gide and Malraux is of enormous technical interest, and their work cannot be properly appropriated if this dimension is ignored. But, when we read *Les Faux Monnayeurs*, it is not the experimentalist in "point of view," but Gide in his role as theorist of the gratuitous act, who interests us most deeply; in the theatre of Pirandello, what we are perplexed and engaged by most profoundly is not the sheer pyrotechnics of his eccentric dramaturgy but the bitter existential comedy, say, of *Right You Are*; and, in a novel like *L'Espoir*, what we feel to be of high significance is not Malraux's adaptation of the techniques of cinematic *montage* but his tragic humanism, his vision of fraternity, and his *mystique* of action. Indeed, it has been more often true than not that the major writers of this century—such figures as Kafka and Lawrence and Mann and Eliot and Auden—have in some deep sense been, as the French say, *directeurs de conscience*, and it is the gravity and the brilliance with which Camus has carried this tradition into the present time that in large measure accounts for the great prestige that his name continues to have among us today. The literature that he produced is a literature drenched in ideas; and his plays and novels impress so deeply because their rhetoric is vibrant with the central themes of the modern consciousness.

Camus' vision is, in other words, an emphatically modern vision: in him we behold the style of the age, and this is so because, for him, the ultimate exigency which man faces in our time is an exigency arising out of a great abdication, a terrible collapse, a tragic death, in the City of God Himself. His

12

work is inspired by the characteristically modern sense that the only anchorage for the human enterprise, therefore, lies somewhere within itself, and that any principles of meaning by which man's universe is to be ordered, he must himself contrive out of the inventiveness of his own untrammelled creativity. He sees the human voyager as utterly alone and with nothing to rely upon except the compass of his own mind and heart. Man must give himself his own directions: it is up to him, and to him alone, to decide where he shall go. It is this image of the human condition that underlies the drastically truncated Pascalianism to be found in the remarkable texts produced by Camus in the last twenty years or so of his life.

It is, to be sure, a sense of life that gained in lucidity and coherence, as he passed from youth into middle age, but it proved its shaping force as early as his first book, the slim collection of lyrical essays that Edmond Charlot published in Algiers in 1937 under the title *L'Envers et l'endroit*. Most of the studies in this book—indeed, all but one of the five—aim at creating a repertory of images that will each incarnate some aspect of the nakedness and vulnerability and solitude and banality that make for man's permanent and irremediable anguish. The essays resemble short stories, and in the first, "L'Ironie," we are concerned, for instance, with the figure of an old woman (whose portrait may owe something to the grandmother who, in Camus' boyhood, lived in the impoverished apartment of his widowed mother in Algiers): she represents, says Camus, "la misère de l'homme en Dieu." Which is to say that hers is a religion without joy or happiness or indeed any real personal validity at all, its sole function being merely to provide some meagre consolation before the frightening imminence of death; and it is suggested that, had she any expectation of recovering from her illness, her rosary and her plaster St. Joseph would quickly fall into disuse. But she is without hope, and so, in her corner of neglect, she despairingly clings to the machinery of her piety and drones out her complaints against the bleak abandonment which is her fate. When the younger members of the family leave her to go out to the cinema in the evening, she clutches her daughter's hand, and a young guest is overcome by the pathos of the spectacle and the occasion—"an old, crippled woman whom they were abandoning to go to the movies." Like the old man whom we also meet in this section of the book, as he futilely attempts to engage some young people in conversation in a café, she is "condemned to silence and solitude"; and, as they both approach the last great emergency of death, "old age comes over [them] . . . like nausea." They are *isolés* who, when they look up, descry only "the vacuous indifferent smile of the sky" and who, when they look back upon themselves, behold only their stark exposure to the hazards of old age and imminent death.

In the second essay, "Entre oui et non," Camus recalls his early years in Algiers and the straitened circumstances in which he and his widowed mother lived together, in poverty and in silence, neither ever managing in any deep way to reach the other or to find in their relationship any relief or release from their fundamental human separateness. Though held together by the primitive power of the filial bond itself, each was a stranger to the other,

14

and neither found in the other the comfort that might have reduced their sense of being strangers in the world.

And in the essays which immediately follow, "La Mort dans l'âme" and "Amour de Vivre," this sense of strangeness and alienation becomes, even more emphatically, the central theme. These are essays in which Camus recalls his experience as a traveller, and what he finds most characteristic of that experience is the special kind of self-dislocation which is induced by one's passage into new scenes and places that are without familiar signs and land-marks. To face a strange and devious landscape is, he suggests, to be given access to some hitherto unrecognized and unexplored dimension of one's own selfhood, for the kind of unheeding inattentive-ness that is induced by a familiar routine and a familiar locale becomes no longer possible. The self is suddenly dispossessed of everything in its environment that customarily permits the con-ventional illusions of security: "the curtain of habit . . . slowly rises and reveals at last the white face of anguish. Man is face to face with himself." In the world of Prague, for example—which is spoken of in "La Mort dans l'âme"—Camus con-fesses to the feeling of disconnection by which he was overtaken, as he struggled with an alien language and with all the difficulties of finding his way about an unfamiliar city. Nor was this feeling of alienation put off, he tells us, when he moved from Czechoslovakia to Italy: indeed, the very warmth and opulence of the Italian landscape bring a depression of their own, since, by their intensification of one's awareness of the grandeur and beauty of the world, they awaken in us, with a new stab of poignancy, a sense of the tragic brevity of man's life and of the terrible cheat that is ultimately practised upon us.

In the second travel essay, "Amour de vivre," Camus expresses again this strain of melancholy, inspired now, in the Balearic Islands of Majorca and Ibiza, by the very bounteousness of the landscape's splendour, which has the effect of reminding the traveller of the bitter fact that it conceals, that ours is "a universe which has no place for us, in which our life makes no sense." And thus, paradoxically, it is the very love of life that brings at last a profound despair about life.

In the final essay Camus makes explicit the duality that underlies the book as a whole and that is alluded to in the *envers* and *endroit* of the title. For, on the one hand, as he says, there are "les hommes et leur absurdité," their poverty and dereliction and helplessness before the cruel contingencies of life; and, on the other hand, opposed to the precarious transiency of the human enterprise, there is the indestructible beauty of the sun and the sky and the sea and of all the great enduring places of the earth. And so, he contends, given this essential rift in the scheme of existence and despite the absence of all ultimate sanctions, we must " 'Live as if . . .'," in exultant commitment to the concrete, sensual materiality of the world. This, he says, "is the sum of my wisdom" which was spoken to him by "the irony which lies hidden at the heart of things."

Now, despite the sternly reticent and austere tone that was already a noticeable feature of Camus' writing, *L'Envers et l'endroit* is, nevertheless, decidedly the work of a very young man. The essays, taken as a whole, are not unified by any developed and coherent view of the world: the one basic observation that they tenuously record is that of the 90th Psalm, that our years are brought to an end as a tale that is told and that our strength is but labour and sorrow, so soon does it pass away. Yet, for all the disjointedness of the book, it does present a first, inchoate statement of what was to be the guiding axiom of Camus' entire meditation on the human problem, that man is "alone, helpless, naked," in a world whose beauty and splendour only emphasize its unshakeable indifference to *l'humaine présence*.

II

In one of the letters collected by Eberhard Bethge into the volume *Letters and Papers from Prison*, the distinguished young German theologian, Dietrich Bonhoeffer, who was executed in Hitler's Germany in the spring of 1945, recognized that "We are proceeding towards a time of no religion at all: men as they are now simply cannot be religious any more."[1] There is no other writer of the present time who gives us a deeper insight into the condition of this new "religionlessness" than does Albert Camus. To contemplate the movement of his thought is to discern anew the causes of the decline of what Bonhoeffer called "the religious premise," and it is also to discern what is most vital and promising in the "religionlessness" that is today so generally a part of our intellectual situation in the Western world.

One of Camus' most sensitive American critics, R. W. B. Lewis, in discussing his "quarrel with God," has expressed regret that it should be marked by such "inaccurate firing."[2] Mr. Lewis means that in part Camus' refusal of Christian theism is a refusal of a doctrine of divine transcendence on which the integrity of the Christian

---

[1] Dietrich Bonhoeffer, *Letters and Papers from Prison*, ed. by Eberhard Bethge and trans. by Reginald H. Fuller (London: SCM Press Ltd., 1953), p. 122.

[2] R. W. B. Lewis, *The Picaresque Saint: Representative Figures in Contemporary Fiction* (Philadelphia: J. P. Lippincott Co., 1959), p. 78.

faith is not really dependent. This may be so, but it cannot be gainsaid that the apologetic which modern intellectuals have usually encountered in theologians has been one which has spoken about God in the manner of a *terra incognita*, as though He were *a* being or person beside or above other beings or persons, and one whose "existence" was a matter of theoretical knowledge. The kind of spatialization of the divine that has sometimes been implicit in supernaturalist theism is, of course, profoundly at odds with the deepest meanings of biblical faith, and what we have also to grant is that it is a frigid and blasphemous monstrosity which the human reason can accept only by committing suicide. This is a God who, since He is *a* being among others, "is bound to the subject-object structure of reality . . . [and is, therefore,] an object for us as subjects. At the same time we are objects for him as a subject. . . . For God as a subject makes me into an object which is nothing more than an object . . . [appearing] as the invincible tyrant, the being in contrast with whom all other beings are without freedom and subjectivity. . . ."[1] This is the God whom Camus knew, and the refusal of whom lies at the root of the melancholy which persists beneath the surface of even his most positive affirmations.

Now, having rejected the ineffectual consolations of an unserviceable supernaturalism and not having envisaged the possibility of a "god above the God of theism,"[2] the question to which Camus addressed himself in his first books was the question

---

[1] Paul Tillich, *The Courage to Be* (New Haven: Yale University Press, 1952), p. 185.

[2] *Ibid.*, p. 186.

as to the basis on which human life is to be sustained against the immense indifference of the world. Early in his book of 1942, *Le Mythe de Sisyphe*, he tells us that "in a universe suddenly divested of illusions and lights, man feels an alien, a stranger. His exile is without remedy since he is deprived of the memory of a lost home or the hope of a promised land." And it was the full implication of this terrible and absurd forlornness of man's estate that he proposed to clarify.

In *Le Mythe de Sisyphe*, man's exiled condition is called "absurd," because it is so completely alien to the mind's deepest desires. For the essential impulse of the human spirit is to behold the world as its real home, to be assured of some basic congruence between its aspirations for intelligibility and the essential constitution of reality. But, in this world, everything is given, and nothing is explained: the mind's hunger for coherence is countered by the irremediable incoherence of existence: "all the knowledge on earth will give me nothing to assure me that this world is mine." And though, in imagination, we touch the fringes of the eternal, we are but the feeblest reeds in nature, engulfed within the infinite opacity of the world. Indeed, the ultimate outrage is the certainty that we will die, and "the cruel mathematics that command our condition" involve us in a tragic calculus that seems, in the end, to make for an absolute nullification of every conceivable value. Hence, the opening sentence of *Le Mythe*—which is one of the most famous sentences in recent literature: "There is but one truly serious philosophical problem, and that is suicide."

The bitter despair that is promised by this opening sentence turns out, however, not to be the predominant stress of the book. It is, indeed, Camus' whole purpose in *Le Mythe* to demonstrate that suicide can be no real solution to the problem of the Absurd. For, if the Absurd results from the clash between the human demand for clarity and justice and "the unreasonable silence of the world," it cannot be resolved by destroying one term in the polarity which gives rise to the problem. "If I attempt to solve a problem, at least I must not by that very solution conjure away one of the terms of the problem": this would be to annul it, not really to solve it. And, what is more, it would be for man to consent to his own defeat, for, in the desperate leap out of the Absurd into the spurious relief of nothingness, he repudiates himself: he consents to his humiliation, himself becomes the agent of it, and, in thus succumbing to his impotence, effectively abdicates his humanity.

So, then, if the ultimate quandary of our existence cannot be resolved by fleeing from existence, our choice must therefore be *for* existence and for the lucidity by which alone we can live in the Absurd with dignity and honour. And not only are we forbidden "the leap" out of the Absurd by self-inflicted annihilation: Camus also castigates any and all other attempts to "leap" out of the human condition, and most especially those that involve an effort to "transcend" the human realm by "[deifying] what crushes [us] and [finding] reason to hope in what impoverishes [us]." For example, Jaspers, Camus says, finds "nothing in experience but the confession of his own impotence and no occasion to infer any satisfactory principle. Yet without justification . . . he suddenly asserts all at once the transcendent . . . and the superhuman significance of life. . . . Thus the Absurd becomes god . . . and that inability to understand becomes the existence that illuminates everything." This is a kind of cheating that he finds not only in Jaspers but in many other modern thinkers—in Kierkegaard, in Shestov, in the religious existentialists generally: and a similar irrationalism he discerns in Husserl and Scheler and the phenomenologists. Here is a family of thinkers who, in the tradition of Tertullian, begin with the obscurantist proposition, *credo quia absurdum est*: that is to say, they begin with "a philosophy of the non-significance of the world": they see with great acuteness "that divorce between the mind that desires and the world that disappoints." Yet they prove the Absurd only to suppress it and to retreat from what they have brought to light. They are bent on escaping from the irremediable antinomies of the human condition: they are unwilling to endure the deserts of the Absurd: so, "starting from a philosophy of the world's lack of meaning, [they end] by finding a meaning and a depth in it." The Absurd is used as a springboard to eternity, and this is an intellectual trick which negates human reason and involves nothing less than "philosophical suicide."

There is, then, no humanly valid way, Camus asserts, of moving beyond the Absurd, of moving beyond the human. So what we must learn to do is to live with lucidity and without hope, nourished only by "the wine of the Absurd and the bread of indifference." "Living," he says, "is keeping the Absurd alive. Keeping it alive is, above all, contemplating it." And this is what the absurd man

22

consents to do: he is a man without nostalgia who consents to live *in* the Absurd, not acquiescently but defiantly, indifferent to the future, refusing all "supernatural consolations" and sustained only by his cold resolve not to relax the posture of rebellion.

Now this ethic of indifference entails a kind of stern hedonism, for, if "this life has no other aspect than that of the absurd . . . then I must say that what counts is not the best living but the most living"—which is to say that the notion of quantity will be of greater ethical significance than the notion of quality. And thus it is that, for Camus, Don Juan is one of the great "heroes of the absurd," for he goes from woman to woman not because he is guided by Ecclesiastes but because, having no hope of another life, he finds it logical to insist on satiety.

In his way of approaching the legend of Don Juan, Camus puts us in mind of the great portrait of the seducer in Kierkegaard's *Either/Or*, for he too insists on an unromantic perspective, refusing to regard Don Juan as a melancholy mystic in quest of an absolute love. He is a man, says Camus, who does not intend to be duped by the Absurd—which is perhaps simply to say that he does not intend to worry about how his life might be given such a pattern and order as might guarantee some genuine self-fulfilment, for he is without the illusion of freedom. And, knowing that beyond this limited universe "all is collapse and nothingness," he is a man who is determined to face the future with utter indifference and "to use up everything that is given." Since, for him, all experiences are equally important or equally unimportant, he takes it as his one rule of life to seek the greatest quantity of

23

experiences and to live them with the greatest possible intensity and passion. "If he leaves a woman it is not absolutely because he has ceased to desire her. A beautiful woman is always desirable. But he desires another, and no, this is not the same thing." In other words, possession, conquest, and consumption are his norms. And he is a "wise man" —his wisdom, however, not being some esoteric *gnosis* of the great tragic hero but being, rather, the wisdom of an ordinary seducer who, not having the merest vestige of any ultimate hope, is simply intent on enjoying this present life to the greatest possible degree. Nor does he have any regrets, for whatever the degree of lucidity he achieves, it never occurs to him to think of changing his vocation or altering his condition.

But Don Juan is not the only exemplary instance for Camus of *l'homme absurde*. The actor, too, is for him a great archetype of "absurd" living, for, as the practitioner of an art of simulation, of appearance, he incarnates the truth that the various fictitious lives he impersonates on the stage are as unreal, as lacking in lasting significance, as his own. So, in a way, his very role as actor represents the absurdity of the general human condition.

In the iconology of the metaphysics of the absurd, the actor's position is, however, somewhat different from Don Juan's. For Don Juan lives through the absurdity of life actually and existentially; whereas the actor is *l'homme absurde* only in a purely formal and analogical way. Yet he is for Camus a most powerfully evocative image, for

He abundantly illustrates every month or every day that so suggestive truth that there is no

absurd — foolish, nonsense

frontier between what a man wants to be and
what he is. Always concerned with better
"acts," he demonstrates to what a degree appearing creates being. For that is his art—to simu-
late absolutely, to project himself as deeply as
possible into lives that are not his own. At the
end of his effort his vocation becomes clear: to
apply himself wholeheartedly to being nothing or
to being several. The narrower the limits al-
lotted him for creating his character, the more
necessary his talent. He will die in three hours
under the mask he has assumed today. Within
three hours he must experience and express a
whole exceptional life. That is called losing
oneself to find oneself. In those three hours he
travels the whole course of the dead-end path
that the man in the audience takes a lifetime to
cover.

So it is no wonder, says Camus, that the Church
has so often regarded the actor as a questionable
figure. For it is his body which is the actor's means
of expression: he must translate everything into
physical and vocal gesture, and his cultivation of
intensity at the level of the physical life presents a
standing challenge to Christianity's tendency to
subordinate the physical to the spiritual. And it is
also in his commitment to the immediacy of the
present moment, the moment that exists on the
stage, and in his protean self-identification with
many dramatic roles that the Church has found a
reality subversive of its whole programme for the
management of life and for the redemption of man.

From Don Juan and the actor Camus turns to a
third *exemplum* of the absurd man: the adventurer

25

or conqueror who, in undertaking some large programme in the historical order, behaves "as if" the one really useful action, "that of remaking man and the earth," were actually possible. Although his is a militant and activist posture, Camus' conqueror, as he is portrayed in *Le Mythe*, is not a mere gangster who plays the game of power simply to satisfy a crude lust for empire and sovereignty. In the section of the book devoted to his portrait, Camus makes him speak on his own behalf and in the tone of a theorist (or even poet) of rebellion who, believing himself to have been "deprived of the eternal," has closed his heart, has chosen to ally himself with time, and has opted for the life of action rather than contemplation. "Between history and the eternal I have chosen history because I like certainties. Of it, at least, I can be certain. . . ." He seeks contact with the spirit of metaphysical insurrection through the decisive historical act, by "plunging into the seething soul of revolutions." But he knows that there are no victorious causes, that, in the face of death, all causes are lost causes: yet he maintains his lucidity, even in the midst of what negates it, determined never to relax the posture of protest and resistance. Like Garcia in Malraux's *L'Espoir*, he intends to "*organize* the apocalypse."

Then, finally, Camus finds the absurd to be crucially instanced in the artist or the "creator," because, though knowing the work of art to be only an impotent artifact, he yet persists in the practice of his craft, thereby exemplifying a type of revolt against the human fate: he is, indeed, among the most absurd of all men.

Perhaps the key sentence in Camus' meditation

on the meaning of art is that in which he says: "If the world were clear, art would not exist": for this is the notion that is central to his whole understanding of the place of aesthetic creation in man's spiritual life. His premise is, of course, the world's absurdity, its defiance of every conceivable system of coherence, and the necessity that we face, therefore, of maintaining *our* lucidity, despite the incomprehensibleness of existence. And it is just here that he locates the great significance of art. For, though it originates in the uselessness of "explanation" and is symptomatic of the mind's deepest ailment, it is far from being any kind of refuge from the bitter truth of our condition: it is, on the contrary, the great way in which *l'homme absurde* faces that truth and mimes the reality of our common fate. The world refuses to yield to the human spirit anything other than the stubborn fragmentariness of concrete phenomena, and the work of art therefore, in so far as it attempts simply to mime the concrete, attests, in its very being, to the impossibility of transcendence. Indeed, the truest work of art, Camus suggests, is that which consents to say the least, which is "devoid of lessons"; and he is the most exemplary of artists who simply "works up appearances and covers with images that which has no reason."

It is, then, Don Juan, the actor, the conqueror, and the artist whom Camus offers as the great models of living in the absurd; and their dilemma is concentrated for him in the mythical image of Sisyphus, who, for having attempted to conquer Death itself, was punished in Hades by being compelled eternally, but unsuccessfully, to push a great rock to the top of a hill. Here, Camus feels, we have the full, grand human thing itself—impotence yet rebellion, overwhelming odds yet resolute endurance, defeat yet victory. He "teaches the higher fidelity that negates the gods and raises rocks. . . . One must imagine Sisyphus happy." It is, to be sure, a very tragic kind of happiness, but happiness it is, nevertheless, for Sisyphus maintains an intense awareness of the grim actuality that confronts him: he is unflinching in the face of his destiny: he knows that he will never reach the summit of his hill, but he never abdicates the struggle. And, in the rugged persistence of his refusal to allow the rock to remain at the bottom of the mount, he remains faithful to that essential *humanum* within himself, loyalty to which will bring a man the only sort of genuine happiness that is possible for humankind—namely, the happiness that comes from not betraying the dignity that belongs to one's nature as a man. He, therefore, *is*, and suggests, by the example of his Passion, that the human spirit may not be utterly exhaustible by the Absurd: at least he proves himself to be stronger than his rock, for "the rock is still rolling."

There is an element of glamorous titanism in all these figures—in Don Juan and the conqueror, in the artist and in the mythical Sisyphus. But Camus cautions us against mistaking the ethic of the Absurd as an aristocratic ethic appropriate only to an élite. He tells us quite plainly that it is lucidity alone that matters and that, in this, an obscure Post-Office clerk can be the equal of a conqueror. Which means that he regards the absurd as something soberly to be faced throughout all the occasions and undertakings of the normal life of man. For—and this is the essential "democracy" of the human situation, as Camus understood it—whether he be a king or whether he be a chimney-sweep, all that any man can count on for his soul's sustenance is the kind of courage that Hemingway liked to call "grace under pressure." And this is something which the conqueror, he believed, can no more take for granted than the Post-Office clerk.

III

It was his first novel, *L'Etranger* (which appeared along with *Le Mythe de Sisyphe* in 1942, though it had been finished a few months before the completion of the essay), that established Camus' international reputation. And here, in the plot and the images of a work of prose fiction, we are made to experience the sensation of the Absurd with a degree of immediacy that is, I think, at no point equally realized in *Le Mythe*; and in Meursault, the little clerk in an Algerian shipping firm, we have one of Camus' purest renderings of the absurd man.

The narrative line of the novel is very simple. Meursault receives word that his mother has died in a home for the aged. So he requests a brief leave from his business firm in order to go to her funeral in the country district in which the home is located. He is unmoved by the occasion and feels nothing other than the mild stupor that is induced by the summer heat. He returns to Algiers on a Friday evening and, the next morning, goes down to the beach for a swim. There he meets Marie, who used to be a typist in his office. After swimming together, they go to a Fernandel film, then back to Meursault's room and bed and the beginning of a liaison. In the course of the summer, after an acquaintance of Meursault's, Raymond, has beaten up his mistress, he consents to testify on his behalf before the police. And, one weekend, while he and Raymond are visiting Raymond's friends, the Massons, at their summer cottage, they encounter this girl's Arab kinsmen on the beach. In a scuffle that ensues Raymond is knifed by one of them. Later, on the afternoon of that same day, Meursault returns to the beach alone, where he finds one of the Arabs lying in the shade. He sees the Arab draw his knife: the light of the blazing sun glints on the steel, and, says Meursault, "I felt as if a long, thin blade transfixed my forehead. . . . I was conscious only of the cymbals of the sun clashing on my skull. . . . Then everything began to reel before my eyes. . . ." And at this moment he reaches into his pocket for the revolver which he had taken from Raymond earlier in the day. "Every nerve in my body was a steel spring, and my grip closed on the revolver. . . . I fired four more shots into the inert body. . . . And each successive shot was another loud, fateful rap on the door of my undoing."

The second part of the book is devoted to the interrogation and the trial. And, throughout the long proceedings, Meursault displays the same indifference that he had shown towards his mother's death. Indeed, it is his behaviour on that earlier occasion by which those presiding over his trial seem chiefly to be outraged, and one feels that he goes to the guillotine not so much for having killed the Arab as for not having wept at his mother's funeral.

Then, at the last, he is visited in his cell by the prison chaplain who comes to talk to him theologically about judgment and redemption, and to offer the comfort of the Christian faith. It is at this moment that Meursault gains a new lucidity which propels him out of his habitual indifference into a violent rejection of what he believes to be the thin ethereality of the chaplain's piety. As he faces the ultimate emergency of his own ordained death, the wan spiritualism of the chaplain's religion, in its conventional otherworldliness and sterile asceticism, strikes him—to use a phrase of D. H. Lawrence's —as really "doing dirt on life." So, as he says:

I started yelling at the top of my voice. I hurled insults at him, I told him not to waste his rotten prayers on me. . . . He seemed so cocksure, you see. And yet none of his certainties was worth one strand of a woman's hair. Living as he did, like a corpse, he couldn't even be sure of being alive. . . . Actually, I was sure of myself, sure about everything, far surer than he; sure of my present life and of the death that was coming. That, no doubt, was all I had; but at least that certainty was something I could get my teeth into—just as it had got its teeth into me.

And it is in the light of this new clarity that he suddenly discerns what is really ultimate in his existence, that

From the dark horizon of my future a sort of slow, persistent breeze had been blowing toward me, all my life long, from the years that were to come. And on its way that breeze had levelled out all the ideas that people tried to foist on me in the equally unreal years I then was living through. What difference could they make to me, the deaths of others, or a mother's love, or his God; or the way a man decides to live, the fate he thinks he chooses, since one and the same fate was bound to "choose" not only me but thousands of millions of privileged people who, like him, called themselves my brothers. . . . All alike would be condemned to die one day. . . .

In this final moment, once Meursault consciously perceives the utter futility of any kind of ultimate hope, it is as if a cloud had lifted: as he abandons himself to "the benign indifference of the universe," he suddenly realizes that his has indeed been a happy life and that he is even happy still. "It was as if," he says, "that great rush of anger had washed me clean. . . ." There is, to be sure, nothing other than this earthly existence, but the joys of this life, he now realizes, he has savoured even more deeply than he had known. He recalls the eternal Algerian summer, the sound of the rippling water at his feet down at the beach, the smooth feel of the water on his body as he struck out, the "sun-gold" of Marie's face—and he knows then that the glory of the world is its own justification. So, like Sisyphus, he is sustained by "the wine of the absurd and the bread of indifference," and he faces his last hour with the serenity of one who has moved forward, if not towards some brave new world, at least towards a calm acceptance of the present dispensation. And his final mood is very nearly the ecstasy of a pantheistic mysticism.

Now, it is just this final transfiguration that fails to prove itself, either in terms of the logic of Camus' thought at this period of his career or in terms of the dramatic logic of the novel. What he succeeds in conveying to us—and with a more pungent vividness than any novelist since Kafka—is the very flavour and sensation that life takes on when (paraphrasing Yeats' famous line) things have fallen apart, when the centre no longer holds, and "mere anarchy is loosed upon the world." In the universe that is inhabited by this obscure Algerian clerk all meaning has been displaced by the absurd equivalence into which all possible choices and actions have been collapsed by the death of God and "the cruel mathematics that command our condition." As Jean-Paul Sartre remarked in his fine review of the book in 1943, one is made uneasy by the very first paragraph. Meursault tells us that

> Mother died today. Or, maybe, yesterday; I can't be sure. The telegram from the Home says: YOUR MOTHER PASSED AWAY. FUNERAL TO-MORROW. DEEP SYMPATHY. Which leaves the matter doubtful; it could have been yesterday.

And we are made uneasy because we sense that we have suddenly entered a place in which the significance of events in time has somehow been cancelled out: "Mother died today. . . . it could have been yesterday." And it could have been the day before yesterday: the lifeless monotone of the speaker intimates that the issue is of no consequence to him. Or, again, when Marie asks him one evening if he'll marry her, he says:

> I said I didn't mind; if she was keen on it, we'd get married.
> Then she asked me again if I loved her. I replied, much as before, that her question meant nothing or next to nothing—but I suppose I didn't.
> "If that's how you feel," she said, "why marry me?"
> I explained that it had no importance really, but, if it would give her pleasure, we could get married right away.

And neither issue matters—neither the day on which his mother died nor whether or not he marries Marie—because, as he reasons at the end of the narrative, the "slow, persistent breeze" that blows in upon him from "the dark horizon of [his] future" levels out all distinctions and thus keeps any one action or experience from carrying more significance than others. He knows, in other words —long before the murder, the trial, and his condemnation—that he is going to die. So, when Raymond offers him friendship, when Marie offers him her love, when his employer offers him advancement, when a priest offers him the consolations of faith, he hunches his shoulders and says in effect, "It's all the same to me: makes no difference much: let it be as you will." And it is the unshakeable taciturnity with which he faces the silence of the world that makes him a "stranger," an "outsider": he will have no traffic with the idols of the tribe, he will not give his suffrage to the illusions of those who cannot bear the cold, bitter stone of truth. What is at issue in the trial is precisely this crime, the scandal of the man he has become, who has no feelings, not even at his mother's funeral. His refusal of the conventional emotions appears to the Algerian populace to be a kind of obscenity.

All this is conveyed with an uncanny shrewdness of dramatic gesture. The fragmentation and incoherence which are the basic onotological facts in Meursault's experience of life are present not simply in the assertions of his own broken rhetoric, but they are also present in the whole style and design of the novel. Recalling Francis Fergusson's definition of the tragic rhythm as a movement from

35

purpose to *passion* to *perception*,[1] R. W. B. Lewis has
very acutely observed that, in the case of *L'Etranger*,
the movement is from a "carefully realized pur-
poselessness through a prolonged absence of
passion to the perception that makes them both
right and appropriate. It is, in short, the absurd
mimesis of the tragic."[2] And not only is the novel's
dramatic structure suggestive of Camus' theme, but
we encounter the abyss of nothingness in the very
structure of his syntax. He wants to tell us that the
dark breeze blowing in upon us from the future
means that we really have no future at all, that all
we have is the tenuity of the present instant. And
this is perhaps most powerfully intimated in Camus'
telegraphically laconic syntax. As Sartre observed
in his brilliant essay on the novel,

> The world is destroyed and reborn from
> sentence to sentence. When the word makes its
> appearance it is a creation *ex nihilo*. The sen-
> tences . . . are islands. We bounce from sentence
> to sentence, from void to void. . . . The sentences
> are not . . . arranged in relation to each other;
> they are simply juxtaposed. . . . [They have]
> neither ramifications nor extensions nor internal
> structure. . . . [They are all] equal to each
> other, just as all the absurd man's experiences
> are equal. Each one sets up for itself and sweeps
> the other into the void.[3]

[1] *Vide* Francis Fergusson, *The Idea of a Theater* (Princeton:
Princeton University Press, 1949), Chapter I.

[2] R. W. B. Lewis, *The Picaresque Saint* (Philadelphia: J. P.
Lippincott Co., 1959), p. 71.

[3] Jean-Paul Sartre, "Camus' *The Outsider*," *Literary and
Philosophical Essays*, trans. by Annette Michelson (London:
Rider & Co., 1955), pp. 38–40.

We are, in other words, in a mute and abandoned universe: in Meursault we have an example of man living *in* the Absurd: this is, as the late Rachel Bespaloff said in her *Esprit* article, "the world of the condemned man,"[1] the world that is portrayed with such poignant eloquence in the early sections of *Le Mythe de Sisyphe*. But, then, in the polemic against Kierkegaard and Shestov and Jaspers and in many other sections of that book it is Camus' main purpose to invalidate all attempts to "leap" from absurdity into any kind of faithful affirmation. Yet this would appear to be precisely what is entailed in Meursault's final reconciliation. For he somehow moves from the sullen hopelessness and indifference in whose grip he is throughout most of the novel to the almost ecstatic affirmativeness of his final mood, and we find it difficult to understand what it is that explains and accounts for the passage. The passionate infatuation with life, the felicity, the sense of blessedness even, that Meursault somehow wrests out of the last hours—this is all quite unprepared for in everything that has gone before: so it not only lacks dramatic cogency and credibility, but it seems also to be unsupported by what were the basic premises of Camus' thought in the early 'forties. But the forlorn, dispirited *isolato* who seeks with his own indifference to match the indifference of the world is a memorable figure, and his story is one of the great philosophical myths in the literature of this century.

[1] Rachel Bespaloff, "Le Monde du condamné à mort," *Esprit*, No. 163, January, 1950.

IV

Two years after the publication in 1942 of
L'Etranger and *Le Mythe de Sisyphe* there appeared
the two major plays of Camus' early period, *Le
Malentendu* and *Caligula*. These are works that, in
a way, bring to a close the phase of his career in
which, following the first books of the 'thirties
(*L'Envers et l'endroit*, 1937; *Noces*, 1939), he was
attempting to explore the full depths of modern
nihilism. And, of the two, it is in the sombre,
operatic brilliance of *Caligula* that we get the most
concentrated resumé of the early preoccupation
with *l'Absurde*.[1]

The young Caligula (who at the age of 25 became Emperor of Rome and whose brief, tem-
pestuous reign is chronicled in Suetonius' *Lives of
the Caesars*) is overwhelmed with grief following the
death of his sister Drusilla, for whom he had conceived an incestuous love. His emotions, however,
are not simply those of grief, but also of rage and
anger and indignation. For Drusilla's death, as he
tells his friend Helicon, is but a symbol of the fact
that "Men die and . . . are not happy." This loss,
in other words, precipitates him into *l'Absurde*, dis-
closes how barren the world is of meaning and how
absolutely death nullifies all human values. And,
perceiving how shallow is the general understanding of this truth, he becomes a kind of missionary

[1] *Caligula*, though not published until 1944, had actually
been written, at least in its first draft, as early as 1938, while
Camus was still living in Algiers.

on behalf of the Absurd, deciding that the service he shall render Rome will be that of making known the metaphysical anarchy that dominates existence: he will wear "the foolish, unintelligible face of a professional god." So he arranges a drama that is intended to be a terrifying simulacrum of the unconscionable arbitrariness of fate itself. His method is the method of terror: he confiscates the property of both the rich and the poor; he murders the children and the parents of his friends; he humiliates and tortures distinguished patricians; he awards prizes to the citizens making the largest number of visits to the Roman brothels; he mercilessly decrees executions; he arbitrarily curtails food supplies for the populace; until finally, his malevolence reaches such insane proportions as to make it obvious that no one is safe.

The lesson that this frenzied pedagogue wants to teach is that the ultimate truth about the world is that it has no truth, and he proceeds to do this by creating a delirious kingdom of violence "where the impossible is king." He organizes a campaign against creation, partly in order to bring home to men the real facts of their condition in this world, and partly as an act of revenge against a remote and criminal deity. His demonic ardour is the perverse asceticism of a man committed to absolute rebellion, and this furious adventure in sabotage does indeed at last begin to have its intended effect of unsettling the easy assumption of Caligula's patrician associates that the world has an order and a meaning which guarantee them some fundamental security. The young poet Scipio is even so far converted, despite the murder of his father by imperial decree, that, when he is invited to join a plot against the Emperor, he refuses, declaring: "I cannot be against him. If I killed him my heart, at least, would still be on his side": for, as he says, "The same flame consumes our hearts." And Caligula's mistress, Caesonia, though she urges a course of moderation, does not really withhold her acquiescence in his programme; whereas Caligula wants to enthrone "the impossible," she would like to see the "possible" given a chance: but they are essentially at one in their disillusion, and thus, in a way, she is without appeal when the time comes for her own destruction at his hands.

Finally, however, this madman provokes a rising wave of revolt which culminates in his assassination. The plot is led by his friend Cherea, who becomes, in the dialectic of the drama, his major opponent. He chooses to join forces with the assassins "to combat a great idea . . . whose triumph would mean the end of everything." He acknowledges that Caligula's philosophy is "logical from start to finish," but the trouble with it, as he says, is that it converts itself into corpses—and, though it cannot be refuted, it must be opposed. He is a man in whom hope is as dead as it is in Caligula, but he silences everything in his heart that is akin to the Emperor; for he is on the side of life, and he knows that Caligula is a prince of the powers of darkness who would make even murder legitimate.

When Caligula is first seen on the stage, he has just returned to Rome, after having been away for three days following Drusilla's death. "His legs," says Camus, "are caked with mud, his garments dirty; his hair is wet, his look distraught." And he tells Helicon that he has been reaching for the moon: "I suddenly felt a desire for the impossible. . . . Really, this world of ours, the scheme of things as they call it, is quite intolerable. That's why I want the moon, or happiness, or eternal life —something . . . which isn't of this world." And he declares that the real significance of Drusilla's death lies in the symbol which it provides of "a truth that makes the moon essential"—the truth that "Men die and . . . are not happy." But Cherea, though he knows human existence to be as precarious and as threatened as Caligula says, does not need the moon: he forgoes the Emperor's Luciferian *dandyisme* and chooses instead to dedicate his own strength to fortifying the reign of man: he wants to give the *possible* a chance.

In the great final scene of Act III the two men, with a certain wariness, approach each other for the last time, Caligula initiating the exchange with the somewhat wistful query, "Do you think, Cherea, that it's possible for two men of much the same temperament and equal pride to talk to each other with complete frankness—if only once in their lives? Can they strip themselves naked, so to speak, and shed their prejudices, their private interests, the lies by which they live?" Cherea replies: "Yes, Caius, I think it possible. But I don't think you'd be capable of it." And this is the signal for the fencing match which ensues, in the course of which Cherea admits his inability to refute the logic of the Emperor's plan of life but insists, nevertheless, that, were the Absurd to be pushed to its logical conclusions, the world would then become "impossible to live in, and happiness, too, would go by the board. And these, I repeat," he says, "are the things that count, for me."

> *Caligula:* So, I take it, you believe in some higher principle?
> *Cherea:* Certainly I believe that some actions are —shall I say?—more praiseworthy than others.
> *Caligula:* And *I* believe that all are on an equal footing.
> *Cherea:* I know it, Caius, and that's why I don't hate you. I understand, and, to a point, agree with you. But you're pernicious, and you've got to go.

Given the insufferable anarchy into which Rome has been thrown, the time, in other words, has come for the Emperor's assassination. And, as this late stage of the action gets under way, he does himself begin to show the signs of an inner disintegration: he shatters a mirror in which he beholds the intolerable image of his own hatefulness: and, at the very end, he acknowledges that he has taken a wrong turning, "a path that leads to nothing." Yet the last words are his: as the assassins fling themselves upon him with their daggers, he—"laughing and choking"—gasps out the cry: "I'm still alive!" And thus, like Melville's Ahab, he spits his last breath back at the Absurd, in frenetic and arrogant defiance.

Nor is it at all strange that one should at this point be put in mind of Melville and of *Moby Dick*, for Camus was careful to set down his conviction that the work of Herman Melville constitutes a "record of a spiritual experience of unequalled intensity"[1]; he regarded *Moby Dick* as *the* exemplary instance in the history of prose fiction of *la création absurde*: it is, he said, "one of the most disturbing myths ever invented about the struggle of man against evil and about the irresistible logic which ends by first setting the just man against creation and the creator, then against his fellow-men and against himself."[2] And when, in the 'forties, *Caligula* was first read and seen in performance by the French public, had it been generally known how deep an influence had been exerted on Camus by this great figure of the American nineteenth century, the broader implications of his Roman play might then have been more firmly grasped. It is natural, of course, that, when the play was first introduced in France, it should have been interpreted in the light of the then recent and tragic experience of the Hitlerian insanity and that it should have been taken as a kind of political allegory: and so indeed it was in part. But the artist who had conceived this fearful pageant was a young man who knew the great account of the fated *Pequod* and of its monomaniac old captain Ahab, and he had therefore read, and doubtless been fascinated by, that moving passage in *Moby Dick* in which Melville tells us that "though in many of its aspects this visible world seems formed in love, the invisible spheres were formed in fright." And, far more importantly than the social and political tragedy that was

[1] Albert Camus, "Herman Melville," in *Les Ecrivains célèbres*, Vol. III (*Le XIXe Siècle-Le XXe Siècle*), ed. Raymond Queneau (Paris: Editions d'Art, Lucien Mazenod, 1953), p. 128.
[2] *Ibid.*

precipitated by the Nazi experiment, it was the absurd hero's invasion of these uncharted and horrific Melvillean regions that Camus was attempting to dramatize in *Caligula*.

It is, indeed, this same metaphysical blackness that constitutes the pervading atmosphere of *Le Malentendu*, which, though Camus' second play, was, at the time of its first performance in 1944, his first stage-piece to be presented in a Parisian theatre. Here he gives us a full development of the story which Meursault discovered on a scrap of old newspaper under the mattress in his prison cell; and, in that version, it goes like this, in Meursault's summary:

> . . . its scene was some village in Czechoslovakia. One of the villagers had left his home to try his luck abroad. After twenty-five years, having made a fortune, he returned to his country with his wife and child. Meanwhile his mother and sister had been running a small hotel in the village where he was born. He decided to give them a surprise and, leaving his wife and child in another inn, he went to stay at his mother's place, booking a room under an assumed name. His mother and sister completely failed to recognize him. At dinner that evening he showed them a large sum of money he had on him, and in the course of the night they slaughtered him with a hammer. After taking the money they flung the body into the river. Next morning his wife came and, without thinking, betrayed the guest's identity. His mother hanged herself. His sister threw herself into a well.

Now it is, of course, the function of this brief passage in *L'Etranger* to be simply an odd bit of documentation of the general absurdity of life: the story in no way strains Meursault's credulousness: he takes it for granted that such things happen, and his only comment is that ". . . the man was asking for trouble; one shouldn't play fool tricks of that sort." And the more elaborate version of the tale that we get in *Le Malentendu* is intended to provide much the same sort of evidence that was originally communicated by the old newspaper clipping in a prison cell; the only departures from the narrative summarized in *L'Etranger* are that Jan, the murdered son in the play, has no child, and he is not bludgeoned to death but is drugged and then tossed into a nearby river. Indeed, there is not a single character in the play who lives outside the realm of the Absurd—even though, as is the case with Jan and perhaps with the old man-servant, there may not always be any highly developed consciousness of the true human condition.

The scene of the play is some central European valley whose situation oppresses Martha, the sister, with a sense of being enclosed and shut-in: it is a dark, dreary, unfrequented place where it is always raining and where one dreams of open spaces by the sea that are bathed in a scorching sunlight which burns out the burden of the soul. And, with this dream in their darkened hearts, and most powerfully so in Martha's, she and her mother have systematically murdered the occasional patrons of their inn for the small sums that could be lifted from their persons, hoping eventually to acquire a hoard large enough to permit them to escape to the South—and to the sun and sea. So, when Jan appears, obviously well-to-do and

45

apparently without connections, Martha's decision is immediate and automatic. "I have come here to bring them my money, and if I can, some happiness," says Jan to his wife Maria, whom he insists on leaving temporarily at a nearby hotel. But she contends that "there's something . . . something morbid" in the whole elaborate scheme of disguise and pretence and postponed recognition that he has planned: "No, there's only one way," she says, "and it's to do what any ordinary mortal would do—to say 'It's I,' and to let one's heart speak for itself." He ought, she tells him, to go to his mother and simply say: " 'I'm your son. This is my wife. I've been living with her in a country we both love, a land of endless sunshine beside the sea. But something was lacking there to complete my happiness, and now I feel I need you.' " Jan, however, cannot be shaken from his purpose: so he leaves Maria behind and, on arriving at his mother's inn, his purpose collides with that of Martha and the mother herself: before he has a chance to disclose his identity he is murdered, and is recognized by his mother and sister only after his death, when Maria comes and tells them whom they have killed. So the drama moves finally towards an unspeakably bitter irony of tangled purpose, the result of which is that Maria is robbed of her husband and Jan of his life and his mother and sister of their restoration to their long-lost son and brother. And thus it is no wonder that Martha, as she angrily contemplates their cruel defraudment, says at last to Jan's grief-stricken widow, just before she takes her own life: "Pray your God to harden you to stone. It's the happiness He has assigned Himself, and the one true happiness. Do

46

as He does, be deaf to all appeals, and turn your heart to stone while there still is time."

It would appear that the central revelation which we are expected to perceive as emerging from the tragic dénouement of *Le Malentendu* is that conveyed by Martha in her grim conversation with Maria at the end, when she says: ". . . it's now that we are in the normal order of things, [for] . . . in the normal order of things no one is ever recognized." And this is a view of the human situation that the structure and atmosphere of the play enforce upon us, unquestionably, with a strangely powerful and memorable intensity. Camus' *décor* is here something that is stripped and bare and utterly simple, with none of the brilliant claptrap of drums and clashing cymbals and royal banquets and plays within plays that marked his stage in *Caligula*: the scene is simply that of an isolated country inn where the staff is prepared for murder. And the action has a simple linearity of structure that carries it forward with a relentlessness and inevitability not unlike that of Sophoclean tragedy: the movement is from the son's return to his mother and sister (with his intention to be their deliverer, and with theirs first to murder and then to rob) through the murder and the too-late discovery of Jan's identity to the final moment of shock and mortification, with its divulgence of "the normal order of things," the bleak wintriness of life in a world in which God is absent and where, as Beckett says in *Molloy*, "all wilts and yields, as if loaded down." It is indeed a stage, controlled by strange laws of dramatic irony and coincidence, which leaves a permanent residue in the mind.

Yet, for all the hallucinative power with which

47

the play establishes its world in the imagination, its form, as many of Camus' critics have remarked, is in many ways incoherent, particularly in the delineation of the major characters. Why does Jan, for example, insist upon the guise of anonymity, instead of immediately identifying himself to his mother and sister, as Maria quite sensibly urges him to do? This is a question that the play never really answers, and thus its fulcral point is couched in the most exasperating—and damaging—ambiguity. Everything, to be sure, would have been altered, had Jan simply said at the beginning, as his wife counselled, "It is I." But this he refuses to do, and for reasons not internal to the dramatic situation but, rather, simply because Camus (as he very nearly admitted[1]) wanted to portray insincerity as being the very reverse of man's only possible right attitude, the denial of his only hope of saving himself in an absurd universe—namely "practising the most basic sincerity and pronouncing the most appropriate word."[2] By taking advantage of Jan in this way he has, however, made his character inexplicable in terms of what is intrinsic to the play itself.

Nor is Martha less opaque than her brother. Why has she converted herself into so unfeeling and ruthless a criminal? Is it because (as she suggests at the end) she has determined to harden herself into stone, in order that, by her own deafness to all appeals, she may offer a kind of resistance to a God whose own happiness consists in being

---

[1] *Vide* "Author's Preface" in Albert Camus, *Caligula and Three Other Plays*, trans. by Stuart Gilbert (New York: Alfred A. Knopf, 1958).

[2] *Ibid.*, p. viii.

hard as stone? Or does she murder simply as a way of winning an escape from her dreary valley to some distant southern region that is bathed in sunlight and close to the sea? And why does she yearn so obsessively for the sun? What is it in her experience of life and in her own nature that accounts for this preoccupation? Again, these are questions which are not clearly and persuasively answered by the logic of Camus' play. And, in one final particular, *Le Malentendu* is often marred by a curious kind of excess of which Camus himself seemed to be obscurely aware, for, in his Preface to the American edition, he assures us that the play "is a work of easy access if only one accepts the language"[1]—but this is, of course, precisely the acceptance that it is frequently most difficult to manage, especially when we are confronted by the mother and the sister who occasionally break out into a kind of stiff, elaborate, overly solemn rhetoric that sounds strangely incongruous against the background of their rural simplicity.

The play, in other words, is not without its formal imperfections; and yet, for all these, it possesses that strangely alchemical power (of Kafka's *Der Prozess*, or Sartre's *Huis Clos*, Beckett's *En attendant Godot*, or Ionesco's *Le Tueur*) to convince the men and women of Camus' generation that the distant and unexampled world which it presents is somehow more real than that which will be read about in tomorrow morning's newspaper.

[1] *Vide* "Author's Preface" in *op. cit.*, p. viii.

V

It is in these early works—in *L'Etranger*, in *Le Mythe de Sisyphe*, in the plays *Caligula* and *Le Malentendu*—that we get what Rudolf Bultmann would call Camus' "sense of existence," his sense of what man is up against in this world. And the crux of the matter lies, as I have been suggesting, in the idea of the world's absurdity. This definition of the circumstances in which the human task has to be carried on does not, in fact, posit any specific hindrance or obstruction: it is, rather, simply the calloused "thickness and strangeness of the world" that constitutes our irremediable burden. *L'Absurde* grows out of the fact that life is filled with meanings that are incomprehensible to man, that existence intransigently resists man's demand for rational coherence, and that man everywhere beholds the evidence of the fragility of his life. God is dead, and the sense of *angoisse*, of *l'Absurde*, springs from the absolute uncertainty as to whether or not there is any effective ontological warrant for the continuance of the human enterprise. The issue is the anxiety of emptiness, of meaninglessness; and the scene that is explored in Camus' early writings is the Abyss of *Nada* in whose servitude human life is caught at the end of the modern period—a world in which Nothing is at the centre, the world of Hardy and Conrad, of Hemingway and Malraux and Sartre.

But, having defined what is centrally problematic in modern experience, Camus, from the mid-'forties on, was attempting to conceive a way of surviving and a stratagem of resistance. Nathaniel Hawthorne once remarked of his friend Herman Melville that "he can neither believe, nor be comfortable in his unbelief." Something similar might be said of Camus, at least to the extent to which, in all of his work of the last fifteen years of his life, he was attempting to find "the means to proceed beyond nihilism." Like Cherea in *Caligula*, he believed that it is man's fate to live without hope and without Grace: yet no thinker of our time has been more alert to the futility of the ethics that modern nihilism has produced. Indeed, Camus' most cutting strictures were reserved for those metaphysical rebels of the last hundred and fifty years who, like Ivan Karamazov, have concluded that, since God is dead, then "everything is permitted." For to legitimatize murder is to have allowed the Absurd to intimidate us into unfaithfulness towards humanity.

It was Camus' most fundamental aim, indeed, to find a way of affirming the human order. He wanted neither the easy infinities of conventional religion nor the Manichaean angelism of the modern nihilist, but rather "a form of order that orders indeed, but leaves reality, every iota of yours and mine, intact—multitudinous, different and free, but together at last."[1] And it was this concern that unified his work of the last fifteen years,[2] giving *La Peste* and *L'Homme révolté* a privileged status

[1] William F. Lynch, S. J., "Theology and the Imagination," *Thought*, Vol. XXX, No. 116 (Spring, 1955), p. 34.

[2] Perhaps the one exception is the collection of stories that forms the body of Camus' last published work in fiction, *L'Exil et le royaume*, in which the preoccupation with the themes of exile and alienation to some extent reaches back to the stress of the earlier books.

among his writings of this period, since it is in these books that we get the most concentrated expression of his basic interest. Here, like Ignazio Silone, he was asking the question as to what action will redeem the time and re-establish the image of man: the focus, in other words, had shifted from an analysis of the Absurd to an analysis of how the world's disorder may be resisted and the life of the human creature rectified and renewed.

The French Roman Catholic philosopher Gabriel Marcel tells us that ours is today a world in which "the preposition 'with' . . . seems more and more to be losing its meaning."[1] But the main lesson of *La Peste* seems to be precisely that our solidarity with one another is the one thing that we cannot possibly fail to recognize in "this meadow of calamity,/This uncongenial place, this human life. . . ."[2] "In an absurd world," says Camus, "the rebel still has one certainty. It is the solidarity of men in the same adventure, the fact that both he and the grocer are baffled."[3] And it is our involvement as men in a common fate that constitutes the principal fact for Camus in his book of 1947.

The setting of *La Peste* is the Algerian coast town of Oran, whose inhabitants begin to notice one day an increasing number of rats in their houses. Before long rats are tumbling out of every hole and cranny in the town and dying by the thousands in

[1] Gabriel Marcel, *The Mystery of Being*, Vol. I, trans. by G. S. Fraser (Chicago: Henry Regnery Co., 1950), p. 28.

[2] Matthew Arnold, "Empedocles on Etna," Act II, *Poetical Works of Matthew Arnold* (London: Macmillan and Co. Ltd., 1901), p. 472.

[3] Albert Camus, "La Remarque sur la Révolte," in the collection *Existence* (Paris: Gallimard, 1945), p. 18.

the streets. Then the inhabitants themselves begin to die of a mysterious fever, and it soon becomes evident to the local physicians that all the horrible symptoms spell bubonic plague. So, after weeks of equivocation on the part of the authorities, it is apparent that there is no other course but to employ the most rigorous prophylactic measures and to place the town in quarantine. It is, then, separated from the rest of the world, and, with the closing of the gates, its people are shut in upon the long ordeal of isolation and suffering with which they have to live throughout almost an entire year.

In his epigraph from Defoe, Camus tells us that "it is as reasonable to represent one kind of imprisonment by another, as it is to represent anything that really exists by that which exists not." And the allegorical nature of the fable is emphasized by the dull, provincial scene and by the dispassionate, matter-of-fact objectivity of tone from which Camus never varies in chronicling the events. When the book appeared in 1947, it was at first supposed, particularly by Camus' French readers, to be a rendering of the experience of the German Occupation. But so narrow a construction of its meaning is, I suspect, possible only if the novel is read without regard for the major consistencies of Camus' thought. Seen in this larger perspective, we cannot fail to discern that the plague itself is really an emblem of everything that twists and betrays and otherwise outrages the human spirit in "this uncongenial place." The dilatoriness of the epidemic's progress is the massive inertia of the world, and its murderous malevolence is the disastrous irrationality of the Absurd itself.

In the gallery of characters whom Camus creates to carry his meaning, we are presented with a variety of responses to the crisis. For the little confidence-man, Cottard, the plague suddenly makes the fear and loneliness that he has known for so many years begin to be bearable; as Tarrou says: "He's in the same peril of death as everyone else, but that's just the point; he's in it *with the others*." He is a hunted man: there is crime in his past; and, were it not for the emergency created by the epidemic, the future for Cottard would be something closed and annulled. But the crisis brings him a kind of ransom or deliverance, for it at once interrupts the normal procedures of justice, thus granting him at least a temporary reprieve, and, in the degree to which everybody is equally threatened by the pestilence, it restores to the outlaw a sense of involvement in the common tide of life: he can once again feel his neighbour to be his brother, and his own suffering is no longer a solitary suffering. So the plague is something with which Cottard wishes to co-operate, and, once its fury begins to lessen, he querulously impugns the validity of the death statistics which testify that the worst is over. Now Cottard, with his shabby little "black-market" operation and his emotional profiteering on human suffering, is, without doubt, an unattractive figure. Yet I suspect that to approach him as merely an object for excoriation is to be inattentive to the pathos of his fear and of his nervous insecurity. When one recalls Camus' own disenchantment about the conventional machinery of social justice, as it was expressed, say, in *Réflexions sur la guillotine* or as it is expressed in *La Peste* by Tarrou, one also suspects that perhaps he would even prefer us to accord a certain limited sympathy to this poor wretch who chose finally to be shot by the police rather than surrender.

Then there is the obscure Civil Service clerk, Joseph Grand, who has been writing a novel for years which never advances beyond an introductory sentence that has been subjected to endless revisions: Grand fights the plague by keeping for the medical authorities a carefully detailed statistical account of its progress, and Camus says, half-whimsically, that he is the real hero of the tale. Though he is stricken by the disease, he manages to survive; and it is a survival of more than the body alone, for, whereas Grand's life had for long been trivialized and emptied of significance by his bondage to the barren routine of his minor post in the bureaucratic machine of Oran, it is his participation in a great action, in a collective effort, that reinvigorates his heart and his imagination— so that, at the end, he burns the great mass of manuscript on which he had recorded the countless versions of that single opening sentence for his projected novel. It is no longer necessary for him to force himself into something resembling genuine imaginative activity: the plague has awakened new places in his heart, and the memory of his beloved wife Jeanne is once again a rich and fecund presence in his soul.

Or, again, there is the Jesuit priest, Fr. Paneloux, who at first responds to the catastrophe by declaring in a sermon that it is a divine chastisement visited upon the citizens of Oran for the purging of their wickedness but who, after witnessing the death-agonies of a little boy, gives up any attempt at a rational theodicy and believes by sheer faith

55

alone. It is apparent that neither the rationalist nor the fideist posture in the priest can be easily accommodated to the basic premises of Camus' novel. Fr. Paneloux is, of course, himself a radical, but his is the radicalism of a traditional supernaturalist faith: he lives outside the realm of the Absurd, and though one may hesitate to say that he is *therefore* beyond the grasp of Camus' imagination, the fact is that the depth and inner complexity of the man are never deeply explored. He is one who unequivocally affirms the absolute sovereignty of a gracious and providential Presence. Indeed, so radical is his faith that he has for long been meditating on the question as to whether a priest has the right to consult a physician; and, in his death, he leads us to feel that he has at last decided that he does not have this right. But, inevitably, such unshakeable trust in a Goodness that lies beyond the woe and desolation of this life could only be understood by the author of *Le Mythe de Sisyphe* as a form of "suicide" or abdication. In a world that seems to be governed not by Love but by Death, this obscure North African priest, in his unquestioning submission to the will of God, seems to be a frigid enigma; and it may be a measure of Camus' own failure to achieve, as a novelist, a certain sort of self-transcendence that Fr. Paneloux is so consistently approached externally and without charity.

Rambert, a Parisian journalist who is stranded in the city, embodies, in the poignancy of his separation from the woman in Paris whom he loves, one of the book's major themes, the powerlessness even of love before the terrors and disasters of history. He is a veteran of the Spanish Civil War, and his experience of various crises throughout the world in the 'thirties has convinced him that one ideology deals no more adequately with the troubles of man than any other. Indeed, he has but one belief, and that is in love, not in the abstract idea of it but in his particular relation to the woman whom he adores and from whom, it seems, once the city is placed under quarantine, he is irremediably separated. No sooner are the restrictions promulgated than he begins to plod away, "calling on all sorts of officials and others whose influence would have weight in normal conditions," hoping against hope that he can somehow get permission to leave Oran. "The gist of his argument was always the same: he was a stranger . . . and, that being so, his case deserved special consideration." But the authorities turn a deaf ear to his pleas; finally, after exhausting himself in fruitless interviews and going the round of all the municipal offices, he falls into a period of sheer lethargy and, in his despair, simply drifts aimlessly from café to café. One day, when he tells Rieux, the chief physician in the plague-infested city, that he has come to like "waking up at four in the morning and thinking of his beloved Paris, the doctor guessed easily enough . . . that this was his favourite time for conjuring up pictures of the woman from whom he now was parted . . . the hour when he could feel surest she was wholly his." Yet, after desperately attempting to arrange an escape from the quarantined city, when at last everything has been made ready for his being smuggled out, Rambert suddenly decides to remain and to contribute his own strength to the struggle against the plague. For he has discovered that no man is an island and that he is himself diminished by the sufferings that have befallen the people in this city, even though he is a visitor and unconnected by personal ties with the inhabitants.

It is, however, Jean Tarrou and Bernard Rieux who carry the heaviest burden of the novel's meaning. Tarrou comes to Oran just a few weeks before the onset of the plague: we do not know from where. Though apparently rootless and unattached, he is a man whose human sympathies prevent his living far from the suffering of men. Once it becomes clear how disastrous is the emergency in Oran, he organizes teams of "sanitary squads" to fight the ravages of the epidemic. As a result of this activity, he is soon thrown close to Bernard Rieux, the leading physician in the town, and, between the two, there grows a deep sense of intimacy and friendship. One evening, after an exhausting day of work, Tarrou suggests to Rieux that they take off an hour "for friendship," and then he tells Rieux something of what his life has been like. He was the son of a public prosecutor, and his father had wanted him also to go into the law. When he was barely seventeen years of age, his father had taken him to court to sit through a murder trial in which he, as prosecutor, was demanding the death penalty. He still remembers the cowering figure of the little red-haired defendant in the dock, and he tells Rieux that he was so filled with horror at the murder that his father in turn, as the representative of official justice, was pleading for that he fled from his father's house, thereafter to devote his life to the subversion of a society which based itself on the death sentence. "I wanted to square accounts with that poor blind owl in the dock. So I became an agitator, as they say. I didn't want to be pestiferous, that's all." But then he found himself in revolutionary movements which themselves invoked the death sentence, and at first, he says, he accepted this as a necessary temporary expedient—till one day he witnessed a man's death under a firing-squad in Hungary and saw the hole that was left in the man's chest, a hole big enough to thrust one's fist into. It was in that moment, he says, that he realized that he had himself been a carrier of the plague which for years he had supposed himself to be fighting. And from that point forward his pacifism became intransigent. He knows, of course, that "we can't stir a finger in this world without the risk of bringing death to somebody . . . each of us has the plague within him; no one, no one on earth is free from it. . . . All I maintain is that on this earth there are pestilences and there are victims, and it's up to us, so far as possible, not to join forces with the pestilences." His path, he says, is "the path of sympathy," and "what interests me is learning how to become a saint . . . without God."

Though one feels that Camus' own vision is expressed more unequivocally by Tarrou than by any of the other characters in his fiction, one also feels that it may be Rieux's modest optimism that most nearly approximates the position to which Camus wanted always to be faithful. Like Cherea in *Caligula*, Rieux, though an atheist, has no taste for atheistical dialectic. The one occasion on which he evinces any irritation with his friend Tarrou is that on which Tarrou asks him if he believes in God. He replies that, of course, he does

59

not, but he also indicates his principled impatience with this kind of question. The really vital point, he says in effect, is that creation as we find it is something to be fought against, and when one joins this fight, then one is on the right road. All I know, he says to Tarrou, is that "there are sick people and they need curing." He has only one certitude, "that a fight must be put up, in this way or that, and there must be no bowing down. The essential thing was to save the greatest possible number of persons from dying and being doomed to unending separation." And, as he says to Rambert, "There's no question of heroism in all this. It's a matter of common decency"—by which, he says, he means simply doing one's job.

So, when Tarrou speaks to him of his interest in learning how to become a saint without God, Rieux bristles slightly and confesses: "Heroism and sanctity don't really appeal to me, I imagine. What interests me is being a man." To which, with beautiful irony, Tarrou replies that he is "less ambitious." Or, again, when one day over the death-bed of the little son of the police magistrate, Monsieur Othon, Fr. Paneloux suggests to Rieux that, in a way, they are partners in working for man's salvation, the doctor replies: "Salvation's much too big a word for me. I don't aim so high. I'm concerned with man's health; and for me his health comes first."

Thus, in Jean Tarrou and Bernard Rieux—and especially in the latter—Camus offers us an image of the kind of virtue, of the kind of holiness, that is possible for man in a time when God is absent. And what is clear is that it is a holiness that consists in a certain kind of resistance or revolt. The fundamental ontological realities, Camus seems to be saying, cannot be altered: the universe is not fully comprehensible and does not answer the human demand for clarity and coherence; there can be no avoiding that final annulment of the human enterprise in the death that awaits every living creature; nor is there even any way of guaranteeing man's protection from the brutal contingencies of nature and of history. But at least we may struggle *for* man and *against* whatever it is that would thwart or defeat or humiliate his humanity. The way, as Tarrou says, is the way of sympathy, of love, of compassion; and, when we see it as our human vocation to cherish and to defend the life of our fellow-creatures, we have then also undertaken what Camus liked to call resistance, for we have set ourselves against a world-order that is indifferent to the hopes and aspirations of the human community.

It is, indeed, the purity of Christ's compassion that explains, I suspect, Camus' profound reverence for the human figure of Jesus. The French critic Roger Quilliot is probably right in saying that "cut off from his divine ascendance, Christ becomes for Camus what he was for Alfred de Vigny, the highest incarnation of . . . human grandeur."[1] He was one who attempted to heal what is broken in human life, to defend mankind against the powers of darkness, and, through the depth and scope of his charity, he became the great exemplar of *résistance*. We cannot, to be sure, change the fundamental order of the world, but we can at least refuse to join forces with it and can thus at least, in a way,

[1] Roger Quilliot, *La Mer et les prisons: Essai sur Albert Camus* (Paris: Gallimard, 1956), pp. 103–104.

revolt against *l'Absurde*. Each of us, as Tarrou says, carries "the plague" within him, but we can at least, through careful vigilance, try to make certain that we do not help to spread it—which is to say that, by dedicating ourselves to the relief of human suffering, we can to some extent contain it and limit it. It is not a matter of heroism but just of common decency. This was the modest optimism that guided Camus' reflections on the human problem during the last years of his life.

VI

When we move from Camus' early works—
L'Etranger, *Le Malentendu*, *Caligula*, and, particularly, *Le Mythe de Sisyphe*—to *La Peste*, it is apparent
that his novel of 1947 signalizes a profound reorien-
tation that was taking place in his thought throughout the 'forties and that is most fully presaged in his
Lettres à un ami allemand which were published by
Gallimard in 1945 (the first two having been written
in 1943). For, in contrast to the author of *Le Mythe*,
the Camus of *La Peste* is concerned to bear witness
to something more ultimate even than the Absurd,
and this is the human spirit itself. This shift in focus
was, as he admits in the *Lettres*, very largely a result
of his experience as a participant in the Resistance
against the German Occupation.

"If nothing had any meaning," said Camus to his
young German friend in December of 1943 in the
second of the *Lettres*—"if nothing had any meaning,
you would be right. But there is something that still
has a meaning." And that something he had come
to believe to be none other than man himself. In
the fourth *Lettre* of July, 1944, he admits to his
former friend that "For a long time we both
thought that this world had no ultimate meaning
and that consequently we were cheated." And he
further admits the baffled unease that he at first
felt, as his German contemporaries began to fill this
void by a kind of anti-human politics whose only
code was that of "the animal world—in other
words, violence and cunning . . . to tell the truth,

I, believing I thought as you did, saw no valid argument to answer you"—except, he says, "a fierce love of justice which, after all, seemed to me as unreasonable as the most sudden passion." He was, in other words, in very much the same position as Cherea in *Caligula*—not being able, that is, to refute his opponent's philosophy which seemed "logical from start to finish," yet not being able to accept a doctrine which converted itself into corpses. But accept it he could not; though he and his German friend had begun from the same premises, they had, finally, undertaken radically different commitments, and the one thing that Camus can say in substantiation of the course which he took is that he simply had "to remain faithful to the world." To be sure, he continues to insist that this world "has no ultimate meaning. But I know that something in it has a meaning and that is man, because he is the only creature to insist on having one. This world has at least the truth of man, and our task is to provide its justifications against fate itself."

The Absurd, in other words, demands revolt: yet revolt, Camus is saying, must itself be subject to some principle of criticism, if it is not to become some form of sheer demonism whose consequences are utterly anti-human. This he believes to have been the case with Nazism: though it was perhaps, in origin, an insurgence of rebellion against the Absurd, the violence of its racial particularism and the ruthless cruelty of its cynical politics converted its revolt against the Absurd into a revolt against man. Thus, he tells his former friend, "you . . . sided with the gods."

Camus here has already travelled far from the

position recorded in *Le Mythe de Sisyphe*. Having been scorched by the agony of France's subjection to the demonic satanism of Nazi Germany, he knows now that Don Juan is not a sufficient guide through the wilderness to which man is condemned. The Nazi experiment has taught him the folly of allowing one's despair to turn into intoxication. In the fourth *Lettre*, it is clear that he has begun to suspect that, if one is to face Evil writ large and disastrous upon the human polity, one must derive some more fruitful conclusion from the Absurd than that "what counts is not the best living but the most living." For this merely quantitative morality is hardly a doctrine that permitted any significant ethical discrimination at all between, say, the Resistance movement and the massive evil which it was opposing. It was out of just this kind of dilemma that Camus, urged on by the exigencies of life in occupied France, began to seek in the early 'forties some principle by means of which the absolute ethical relativism of an "absurd" metaphysic might be modified towards a more genuinely humane end.

It is in the brilliant book that he produced in 1951 on the history of resistance (or "rebellion"), *L'Homme révolté*, that we get the most explicit rendering of this phase of his thought. Here, as in *La Peste*, Camus appears as the celebrant of the human communion, and a communion that is itself established by and in "rebellion." He suggests that the "slave who has taken orders all his life [and who] suddenly decides that he cannot obey some new command" furnishes perhaps the purest instance of rebellion. For when he says "No, you are going too far," he is saying "that there is something in him which 'is worth while . . .' and which must be taken into consideration," that for him to do what he is now ordered to do would be for him to consent to a violation of that in him which makes him a man. He acts, in other words, "in the name of certain values ... which he feels are common to himself and to all men. ... It is for the sake of everyone in the world that the slave asserts himself when he comes to the conclusion that a command has infringed on something in him which does not belong to him alone, but which is common ground where all men—even the man who insults and oppresses him—have a natural community." And thus it is, as Camus says, that, when a man rebels, he "identifies himself with other men and so surpasses himself. ..." Rebellion, then, in the widest sense, "goes far beyond resentment," for not only does it reveal "the part of man which must always be defended," but it also reveals some essential respect in which the human individual is involved in the family of mankind. "I rebel, therefore we are."

The trouble, however, with the great strategists of rebellion in the modern period is, Camus felt, that whether, out of a metaphysical radicalism, they have rebelled against the human condition itself, or whether, out of a social radicalism, they have rebelled against humanly perpetrated injustice, they have tended, in all instances, to ignore the idea that is most basically involved in the logic of rebellion, the idea of *mésure*, of balance, of moderation. If one turns to the tradition of metaphysical rebellion— the tradition of Sade and Lautréamont, of Rimbaud and the Surrealists, of Feuerbach and Nietzsche—one encounters a type of rebel whose belief that God is dead convinces him that man is absolutely free and entitled therefore to do anything that promises to hasten the establishment of the dominion of man. And if one turns to the tradition of historical rebellion—the tradition of Rousseau and Saint-Just, of Hegel and Bakunin, of Marx and Lenin—one encounters a type of rebel who also believes that God is dead and who concludes that history is, therefore, to be "written in terms of the hazards of force." What is tragic in each case is that, given the desacralization of life in the modern period, a rebellion that was initiated *for* man turns in the end *against* man, its demonized purposes being consecrated in blood. What is lost is the *mésure* which might make such demonic fanaticism on behalf of any absolute appear impossible, whether it be the dream of absolute freedom or the dream of absolute justice. This is Camus' critique of the major programmes of rebellion that have been executed since the eighteenth century.

Yet, though no orthodox apologist of our time has been more expert than Camus in discerning the fetters that modern secularism has forged for the human spirit, it is significant that he did not conclude that "rebellion" itself has been invalidated. On the contrary: he believed that our age is irretrievably *désacralisé* and that rebellion, therefore, remains "one of the essential dimensions of man." Even in his last years Camus never repudiated the basic lesson of *Le Mythe de Sisyphe*. To be sure, he did not any longer like to think of himself as an atheist, for, as he said in *Le Monde* in 1955, irreligion had come to strike him as entailing an unseemly kind of presumptuous vulgarity; moreover he wanted to avoid Ivan Karamazov's conclusion that "everything is permitted," wanted, in other words, to go "beyond nihilism." And it is in his attempt to do this, by reinstating a principle of *mésure*, that he claims to have achieved a new stance in the history of modern rebellion.

Now by *mésure*, by the idea of "limit" or "borderline," Camus meant something quite simple: he meant that rebellion can never be for the sake of total freedom (whether for Sade's aristocrat of libertinism or the Romantic dandy or the Nietzschean Superman or the Marxist proletarian or for anyone else), and that it serves humanity only when it "puts total freedom up for trial" and acknowledges that "freedom has its limits wherever a human being is to be found—the limit being precisely that human being's power to rebel. . . . The rebel undoubtedly demands a certain degree of freedom for himself; but in no case, if he is consistent, does he demand the right to destroy the existence and the freedom of others. He humiliates no one. The freedom he claims, he claims for all; the freedom he refuses, he forbids everyone to enjoy. He is not only the slave against the master, but also man against the world of master and slave."

The logic, then, of true rebellion, as Camus understood it, forbids any principle or doctrine that promises to legitimize murder even as a temporary expedient, and this is so, he says, because "rebellion, in principle, is a protest against death." Yet Camus was no conventional pacifist, for he recognized that, the world being as it is, were the rebel absolutely to refuse to kill or lie, he would be "renouncing his rebellion and accepting, once and for all, evil and murder. But no more can he agree to kill and lie, since the reasoning which would justify murder and violence would also destroy the reasons for his insurrection. Thus the rebel can never find peace. He knows what is good and, despite himself, does evil. The value that supports him is never given to him once and for all; he must fight to uphold it, unceasingly." Like Tarrou, he can at least "put his conviction and passion to work at diminishing the chances of murder around him." In thus dedicating itself to a relative justice, rebellion may prove that it is neither mere resentment nor some form of disguised imperialism but "love and fecundity" and compassion; it is at this "meridian of thought" that the rebel "rejects divinity in order to share in the struggles and destiny of all men."

VII

From the two central books of his career (*La Peste* and *L'Homme révolté*) Camus emerges, then, in the line of Antoine de Saint-Exupéry and André Malraux, as a great French poet of *fraternité* for an age that has known the malaise of the Absurd. Throughout his career he remained a poet of *rébellion*, but, in the last fifteen years of his life, there was a noticeable deepening of his concern that the act of revolt should not so generalize itself as to betray the human sodality, and so make the rebel's last state worse than the first. This is the dominant interest in *L'Etat de siège* (1948) and in *Les Justes* (1950), the two plays which immediately preceded *L'Homme révolté* and which anticipate in the concrete terms of dramatic action many of its central themes—just as the earlier plays, *Caligula* and *Le Malentendu*, had embodied the ideas of *Le Mythe de Sisyphe*.

L'Etat de siège was first produced in the autumn of 1948 by Jean-Louis Barrault at the Théâtre Marigny, and though by no means a popular success, it was, in its dramaturgy, the most ambitious theatrical venture that Camus had ever undertaken, with a musical score by Honegger and a stage-décor by the painter Balthus, the arts of mime and burlesque, the devices of monologue and conventional dialogue, ingenious lighting and aural effects and the simultaneous presentation of many scenes being all combined into a spectacle more showy and brilliant even than that of *Caligula*. The setting is the Spanish city of Cadiz, over which, as the play opens, a comet (audibly) passes, a portent that causes great popular consternation. Since "good governments are governments under which nothing happens," the Governor informs the populace that "nothing has occurred to justify alarm or discomposure" and that they are even to deny that a comet has ever risen on the horizon. But when, in the market place, we begin to hear the thud of the falling bodies of those who have been mysteriously and fatally stricken, it is apparent that disaster is at hand; and it is soon impossible to deny that the city has been overtaken by a deadly plague. Indeed, Camus himself, overtaken, it seems, by an uncontrollable allegorical passion, chooses to put the Plague into his cast of characters, this blustering and sinister presence appearing in the city shortly after the epidemic gets under way, being accompanied by a young woman who is his secretary.

The Plague immediately sets to work, with the help of his secretary, to organize lists of the inhabitants, then directing her to tick first one and then another off—and no sooner does her mark go down into her notebook than the thud of a falling body is heard: ". . . from today," says the Plague, "you are going to learn to die in an orderly manner."

Until now you died in the Spanish manner, haphazard—when you felt like it, so to say. . . . Yes, you muffed your deaths. A dead man here, a dead man there, one in his bed, another in the bull ring—what could be more slovenly? But, happily for you, I shall impose order on all that. There will be no more dying as the fancy takes you. Lists will be kept—what admirable things lists are!—and we shall fix the order of your going. Fate has learned wisdom and will keep its records. You will figure in statistics, so at last you'll serve some purpose.

It is not surprising that the Plague should appoint as his chief lieutenant the local iconoclast and wiseacre, Nada, the self-appointed mocker of Cadiz philistinism and of all the established pieties. For Nada's part, in the total design of the play, is to represent that despair grown intoxicated with itself which Camus was attacking in *Lettres à un ami allemand*. "Suppression—that's always been my gospel," he says. "But until now I had no good arguments to back it up. Now I have the regulations on my side." So, dreaming of a total "suppression," wanting to annihilate everything since Nothing "is the only thing that exists," he makes the Plague a most willing and efficient henchman.

The young medical student Diego is the character who finally emerges as the man with sufficient strength to rally the forces of revolt. He, like all the other citizens of the town, is at first simply terrified by the kind of delirious violence which the Plague enacts in the name of law, with its suppression of freedom, its demand that men should betray one another, its fraudulent rhetoric, and its venomous and endless assassinations. But at last the emotion of fright is overborne by the more powerful emotion of disgust at the obscene capriciousness with which human life is being destroyed. When the Plague's secretary discovers Diego in the act of attempting to escape from the city, instead of cowering before her in grovelling abjection, having been tried beyond the point of further endurance, he flings into her face his outrage, his anger, his indignation. And she, having grown weary of killing and having come, as she admits, to have a "soft spot" for him, confides that the Plague's whole system "has a weak point. . . . As far back as I can remember the machine has always shown a tendency to break down when a man conquers his fear. . . . I won't say it stops completely. But it creaks and sometimes it actually begins to fold up." In other words, once a man ceases to be afraid, the Plague then ceases to have any power over him—and when that time comes, it is pointless for the Plague to order his secretary to scratch the man's name off her list: the thud of a falling body will not be heard.

The moment has come for the prophecy, that a wind blowing from the sea would signalize the city's liberation, to be fulfilled. It is the moment when Diego, heartened by the secretary's disclosure, begins to urge his fellow townsmen to join him in an act of revolt. The play then quickly moves towards the great scene of confrontation between Diego and the Plague, who holds Diego's fiancée Victoria as a hostage. The Plague proposes a bargain: Victoria's life for the liberty of Cadiz: "I'll give you that girl's life and let you *both* escape, provided you let me make my own terms with this city." But Diego refuses, and, in exasperation, the tyrant cries out: "You fool! Don't you realize that ten years of this girl's love are worth far more than a century of freedom for those men? . . . No one can be happy without causing harm to others. That is the world's justice." But Diego persists in his rejection of a logic that would permit him to purchase a private

73

fulfilment at the expense of the city's enslavement; to the Plague's definition of "the world's justice," he simply replies: "A justice that revolts me and to which I refuse to subscribe." He chooses, in other words—like the Camus of the *Lettres à un ami allemand*—"to remain faithful to the world," to "the truth of man": he will not side with the gods, for the supreme and single *mésure* to which he gives his suffrage is the human community itself, and to allow his revolt to be turned into a betrayal of his brethren would be for him to transgress the one limit to which he owes absolute obedience. Thus it is that in the young medical student of *L'Etat de siège* Camus embodied that spirit whose tough humaneness he counted on to withstand not only the rampant oppressiveness of political tyranny (the Plague) but also the rampant self-destructiveness of a self-intoxicated nihilism (Nada). Diego is, in other words, the *exemplum* that Camus offers in this play of the rebel doing what is pleaded for in the great final section of *L'Homme révolté*—namely, going "beyond nihilism," in fidelity to the human communion.

It is a similar preoccupation with the morality of *rébellion* which is at the heart of *Les Justes*, the play which was produced for the first time by Paul Œttley at the Théâtre-Hébertot in Paris in December of 1949 and which is modelled very closely on Boris Savinkov's account of Socialist terrorism in Moscow in 1905.[1] The particular movement with which Savinkov was affiliated was the Organization for Combat of the Socialist Revolutionary Party, and the focal point of his book is his narra-

[1] *Vide* Boris Savinkov, *Souvenirs d'un terroriste*, trans. by Bernard Taft (Paris: Payot, 1931).

tive of the group's plot against the Grand Duke
Sergei Alexandrovitch. Two members of the organization, Voinarovski and the student Kaliayev,
were selected to toss a bomb into the carriage of the
Grand Duke as he drove to the theatre on the
second day of February. But, as the carriage passed
the spot where Kaliayev was stationed, he, whose
assignment it was actually to throw the bomb,
could not bring himself to do it, for the Grand Duke
was accompanied by the Grand Duchess and their
little niece and nephew, and this was an eventuality
that had not been anticipated in the group's calcu-
lations. His colleagues afterwards agreed with
Kaliayev, that he was right not to have taken the
lives of innocent children. So they set up a new
plan to kill the Grand Duke two days later when,
as they knew, he would again be driving to the
theatre, and, on this second occasion, the assassination, encountering no obstacles, was successful.
Later, in prison, Kaliayev refused to purchase his
freedom by informing on his fellow conspirators;
nor would he be moved by the Grand Duchess's
appeal that he submit himself to the Church's disciplines of contrition and penance. For, having taken
a human life in what he believed to be a just protest against the tyrannous oppressiveness of the
Russian Establishment, he was insistent that he
should pay with his own.

Now, as he tells us in *L'Homme révolté*, Camus had
the highest admiration for "the men of 1905," for
nowhere else in the history of modern terrorism
could he find assassins in whom the moral imagination conducted so sensitive an inquiry into the question as to whether murder, in any circumstances,
could be justified as a technique of revolt. Indeed,

these were, he says, the *meurtriers délicats*, the fastidious assassins, for they never forgot that, prompted by whatever motives, the destruction of human personality does itself increase the burden of man's woe and is therefore something that must cause the wielders of bombs and revolvers the profoundest unease and chagrin. In *L'Homme révolté* Camus recalls, for example, that Savinkov decided on one occasion, as he was escaping from a Czarist prison, "to shoot any officers who might attempt to prevent his flight, but to kill himself rather than turn his revolver on an ordinary soldier." Of Dora Brilliant, another terrorist, he recalls that Savinkov said that "terror weighed on her like a cross" and that he said of Rachel Louriée that, though she believed in terrorist action, "blood upset her no less than it did Dora." And he cites numerous other instances in support of his contention that, in the history of modern revolutionary action, these people of 1905 represent a truly remarkable highmindedness, a moral nobility that was a consequence of the fact that, though revolution was for them "a necessary means," it was not "a sufficient end"; though they found murder necessary, they also found it to be inexcusable. "History offers few examples," says Camus, "of fanatics who have suffered from scruples, even in action. But the men of 1905 were always prey to doubts. The greatest homage we can pay them is to say that we would not be able, in 1950, to ask them one question which they themselves had not already asked and which, in their life or by their death, they had not partially answered." When Voinarovski declared in his turn: "If Dubassov is accompanied by his wife, I shall not throw the bomb," he was expressing what Camus found to be characteristic of the entire movement—namely, the profound self-abnegation and the fastidious consideration for the lives of others which mark that *sophrosyné*, that moderation, in the power of which *rébellion* can alone hope to be delivered from its own desperateness.

It is not surprising, then, that Camus should have found in Savinkov's memoirs the material for what is perhaps his most moving work for the theatre. The character Boris Annenkov is modelled directly on Savinkov himself, as is Kaliayev on the original, Dora Dulebov on Dora Brilliant, and Alexis Voinov on Voinarovski. And the central line of the play's action adheres closely to the actual sequence of the original events. In the opening act the terrorists (Dora, Annenkov, Stepan Fedorov, and Kaliayev) are together in a sparsely furnished Moscow apartment, where they review the last details for the Grand Duke's assassination which is to be carried out by Kaliayev; in the second act, he returns with the news that the plan could not be executed because of the presence of the Grand Duke's nephew and niece in the carriage. Stepan, grown irascible after years in prison and bearing on his body the marks of the lashings he has suffered, is infuriated by Kaliayev's idealistic temporizing. "Not until the day comes when we stop sentimentalizing about children," he says, "will the revolution triumph, and we be masters of the world." Dora reminds him that "When that day comes, the revolution will be loathed by the whole human race." But his brutal realism is unmoved. Annenkov, however, speaks for all the others when he asserts that the slaughter of the children would have served no purpose: so it is decided to make another attempt in two days' time, and the second act closes with Stepan sneering at what he believes to be the stupid scruples of his associates in terror. In the third act the conspirators gather once again in the same apartment; then Annenkov and Kaliayev, who are to perform the deed, depart, and, at the close of the act, Dora peers through the window and describes the event as it occurs in the street below. The fourth act takes place in Kaliayev's prison cell where both the police chief Skuratov and the grieving Grand Duchess attempt in various ways to elicit from him a renunciation of the deed, Skuratov by promising an amnesty for information on the fellow conspirators, and the Grand Duchess by invoking the dogmas of the Christian faith. But, as we learn in the final act which is very largely given over to Stepan's account of the execution as he witnessed it, Kaliayev, to the very end, remains faithful to his comrades and to their vision of the future.

Now, in the unfolding of this action, there are several scenes which are of focal importance. The first of these is, of course, the terrible *agon* in Act II in which the chief contestants are Stepan, on the one side, and Kaliayev and Dora, on the other. Stepan's passion for an abstract justice and an abstract future has destroyed in him all scruples about means, and he regards the sense of honour and responsibility that led Kaliayev to refrain from murdering innocent children as merely luxurious self-indulgence: he will not complicate the pragmatic issue of expediency and success with fastidious moral considerations. And when Dora cries out: "Even in destruction there's a right way and a wrong way—and there are limits," Stepan, with equal passion, vehemently declares: "There are no limits!" But this is a fanatical ruthlessness that leaves Voinov and Annenkov and the others aghast with horror. And Kaliayev speaks for them all, when he says:

> Killing children is a crime against a man's honour. And if one day the revolution thinks fit to break with honour, well, I'm through with the revolution. If you decide that I must do it, well and good; I will go to the theatre when they're due to come out—but I'll fling myself under the horses' feet.

What, in other words, he refuses to do is to brutalize his fellow human beings for the sake of an uncertain and unknown future: ". . . those *I* love are the men who are alive today . . . it is for them I am fighting, for them I am ready to lay down my life." And though he must sometimes take the part of assassin, he will not be a murderer—a distinction he insists upon. There is, in short, a *mésure*, a limit, which must not be transgressed.

It is precisely this idea of limit, of a border-line beyond which a man of honour does not trespass, that Skuratov is incapable of understanding, as is shown in the great scene of his confrontation with Kaliayev. His is a mind that knows only the simplest logic, and he ridicules what he takes to be the illogic of a terrorist whose ideal permits him to murder a Grand Duke but which makes him balk at murdering children. "If an ideal balks at murdering children, is one justified," he asks, "in murdering a Grand Duke on its behalf?" But, of course the only answer which Kaliayev could give to this question is one which would entail the notion of *mésure* that the police chief, in his commitment to a simple common-sense ethic, has dismissed out of hand.

Indeed, what we feel most strongly in the moving encounter between Kaliayev and the Grand Duchess at the end of Act IV is, again, his fidelity to the idea of *mésure*. The Grand Duchess, in her sorrow, now views the world as a "desert," as a place "empty" and "cruel," and, inevitably, as she faces her husband's murderer, she identifies him with the blighting forces. Yet though she could not be expected to regard Kaliayev differently, it is, ironically, just this view of the world as a "desert" that, in his own way, Kaliayev resists; Stepan is prepared to make a desert in order that Russia may some day be "a land of freedom that will gradually spread out over the whole earth": but Yanek, though he is ready to shed blood, despises murder. As he says in his great scene with Dora in Act III, "I can see the vileness in myself . . . I've got to kill —there are no two ways about it. But . . . I shall go beyond hatred."

Both *L'Etat de siège* and *Les Justes*, then, particularly in the persons of Diego and Kaliayev, give us images of the rebel "at the meridian." Both plays are to some extent disfigured by a certain rhetorical bombast which, as Albert Sonnenfeld has recently remarked with some irritation in a brilliant essay on Camus' dramaturgy,[1] is consistently character-istic of his work for the theatre. But both are plays which speak powerfully of the honour and the generosity and the "strange form of love" which are

[1] *Vide* Albert Sonnenfeld, "Albert Camus as Dramatist: The Sources of His Failure," *The Tulane Drama Review*, Vol. V, No. 4 (June, 1961), pp. 106–123.

ingredients of true rebellion; and, in speaking also of the necessity of rebellion being consecrated in moderation and in the acknowledgment of *la mésure*, they summarize, together with *La Peste* and *L'Homme révolté*, one of the central themes of Camus' thought.

VIII

Christian students of Camus' work have tended generally to go too far in their reaction to *La Chute*, reading it as a kind of gloss on the Pauline theology of the Fall, and thereby trying to suggest that this novel represents a major departure from the basic stress of his thought. It may be, of course, that, through this embarrassingly acute analysis of pharisaism (in the person of the protagonist, Jean-Baptiste Clamence), Camus was to some extent, as R. W. B. Lewis suggests, groping "toward a new basis for solidarity with his fellows: to what might be called the fellowship of those ashamed, the democracy of the guilty."[1] But I suspect that we shall be closer to the truth about *La Chute*, if we approach it in the manner that Camus himself recommended, as a satirical study of a perverted and unhealthy kind of *solidarité*. It is not that Camus was without a doctrine of sin, as I shall shortly emphasize; the issue is rather perhaps his distaste for a definition of what is unitary in the human community in terms of a principle of evil. Rieux tells us at the end of *La Peste* "what we learn in a time of pestilence: that there are more things to admire in men than to despise." But Clamence tells us precisely the opposite, that there is in the human soul nothing but malice and brutish nastiness. And it is through his twisted misanthropy, I suspect, that Camus wanted to complete the dialectic of his message, by presenting an inversion of the heroism

[1] R. W. B. Lewis, *op. cit.*, p. 107.

(which is not so much heroism as simply common decency) that he had theoretically expounded in *L'Homme révolté* and that he had dramatized in various ways in *La Peste*, in *L'Etat de siège*, and in *Les Justes*.

In the intense and bitter monologue that Clamence delivers to a nameless acquaintance whom he meets in an Amsterdam bar, he reviews his brilliant legal career in Paris and the handsome liberality with which he defended the benighted and the penniless, bestowing his charity on the needy and lending his assistance to the unfortunate. "I freely held sway," he says, "bathed in a light as of Eden. Indeed, wasn't that Eden, *cher monsieur*: no intermediary between life and me?" But, as he says, there came a time when all this was overturned, for, one evening as he was walking along the banks of the Seine, he heard a drowning woman's terrified cry for help coming out of the darkness, and he ignored it. From that point onwards, he says, the discovery of his own cowardice slowly led him to the realization of how false and farcical had been the beneficent role that he had hitherto been playing. His charities had simply been a way of winning a sense of superiority over people—but, once this was shattered, he began to feel himself a *pauvre type*, and it becomes apparent that his only way of enduring the wound to his pride was to become what he calls a "judge-penitent." That is to say, amidst the foggy gloom of Amsterdam, he now satisfies his need for condescension by gloatingly convicting others of the guilt that festers in his own soul. The more he accuses himself the more, he believes, he has the right to judge other men, and thus the doctrine of sin becomes an instrument of aggrandizement and exploitation. In other words, he (Jean-Baptiste), like his ancient forbear, is a voice crying (*clamans*) in the wilderness, but, unlike the man who entered Judaea, his is a prophecy that promises not salvation but debasement and humiliation. So Camus, in *La Chute*, was not flirting with any kind of neo-Jansenism, as some of his Christian readers have supposed, but was rather intending to exhibit the kind of morbid perversion of *solidarité* that may be promoted by a soured Manichaeism.

And whether Jean-Baptiste is called a Manichaean or a nihilist does not greatly matter, for, in the end, it comes to much the same thing: like that bilious and exacerbated little cypher whom we meet in Dostoievski's *Letters from the Underworld*, his dominant emotion is one of hatred and contempt for his fellow men, and, with him, the accusation of self is but a pretext for launching such an attack on the human community as will have the effect of subverting all values, all established pieties, indeed all confidence in·man's capacity for truth and decency. Of all the admissions which he makes about himself the one which is perhaps most revealing is that in which he says: "I, I, I is the refrain of my whole life. . . ." And not only everything he says but the very form of the novel itself is calculated to convince us that this is so. There is, presumably, an interlocutor by whom Jean-Baptiste is confronted; but we do not hear this second presence directly—and, once we have grasped the real fibre of the *juge-pénitent*, we begin to feel that the interlocutor is never heard simply because Jean-Baptiste is too much of a bully to allow him to be heard and is too intent on using his doctrine of universal guilt to bludgeon this person into some definitive act of self-abnegation. "With me," as he says, "there is no giving of absolution or blessing. Everything is simply totted up, and then: 'It comes to so much. You are an evildoer, a satyr, a congenital liar, a homosexual, an artist, etc.' Just like that. Just as flatly. In philosophy as in politics, I am for any theory that refuses to grant man innocence and for any practice that treats him as guilty. You see in me, *très cher*, an enlightened advocate of slavery." But it is a slavery to which he does not submit himself, for, despite all his confessing, he is careful, as he says, never to accuse himself crudely. "No, I navigate skillfully . . . in short, I adapt my words to my listener and lead him to go me one better." Which is Jean-Baptiste's way of exempting himself from judgment, of coming out better than the next fellow, and thereby of permitting everything to himself. And this, as he admits, is what is most essential for him—"being able to permit oneself everything, even if, from time to time, one has to profess vociferously one's own infamy." So it is that a Manichaean premise brings him round to the nihilistic freedom of Ivan Karamazov—"Everything is permitted": and this is not a logic which makes any room at all for *la mésure*. In short, Jean-Baptiste Clamence is to be viewed as representing in the universe of Camus' fiction the absolute antithesis of the true rebel.

La Chute, which in length is scarcely more than a *novella*, was first planned as part of the collection of stories that Camus published in 1957 under the title *L'Exil et le royaume*. Had it been somewhat briefer, it might well have entered into that volume to form an interesting contrast with such pieces as

"La Pierre qui pousse" and "Les Muets." For, whereas Camus in *La Chute* is dissecting and evaluating a kind of rampant egoism that is destructive of the human communion, in these stories he is once again celebrating, as in *La Peste*, the sacrament of the brother as the single means of grace and hope of glory. "La Pierre qui pouisse," for example, tells of a French engineer, D'Arrast, who has come to Iguape to build a bridge. Here he meets a native, a mulatto ship's cook, who, in gratitude for his survival of a shipwreck, has vowed to carry on his head a great slab of stone in a ceremonial procession to the church, and there to place it at the feet of Christ. But on the day when he attempts this, he labours and labours, and staggers, and finally collapses under the great weight, in tears, "defeated, with his head thrown back"— whereupon D'Arrast picks up the stone and carries it himself, not to the cathedral but back to the little hut in which the man lives. "And there, straightening up until he was suddenly enormous, drinking in with desperate gulps the familiar smell of poverty and ashes, he felt rising within him a surge of obscure and panting joy that he was powerless to name." Refusing, in other words, to perform an act of Christian oblation, he finds his fulfilment in taking upon himself the burden of a fellow human being and in thus serving what the late Charles Williams called the Companionship of our Coinherence.

In the beautifully composed little story called "Les Muets" M. Lassalle, the proprietor of a small cooper's shop, at a time when cooperage is shrinking with the building of great tankers and tank trucks, refuses to grant his workmen the wage-increase that they so desperately need because of rises in living costs. So they strike. But, having no financial reserves to see them through the strike, they are forced to return to the shop after only a few days' stoppage of work. On the morning of their return, to their great surprise, they find that the doors of the shop are closed. This had never been so before; but M. Lassalle wants to emphasize that he has the upper hand. Only after their arrival does he allow his foreman slowly to push open the heavy doors on their iron rails. And, as they enter the shop, they are silent and humiliated, "furious at their . . . silence, but the more it was prolonged the less capable they were of breaking it." Then, during the course of the day, M. Lassalle's little girl suddenly becomes critically ill, and, in the late afternoon, as the men are preparing to return to their homes, M. Lassalle comes into their washroom, dishevelled and racked with anxiety about his child. They feel his sorrow, and their first impulse is to give their sympathy to the distraught father; but they are still unable to break the silence into which they had been plunged by the humiliation that they had suffered at his hands at the beginning of the day. So, having sinned against the fraternity that is constituted by the little shop (not because he had been unable to increase his workmen's wages but because he had calculatedly submitted them to a cruel snubbing), the man goes out, uncomforted and unsustained by the encouragement by which he would have been upborne had his previous behaviour permitted his fellow human beings to give him the solace which their natures craved to offer.

This, then, is the one type of story in *L'Exil et le*

royaume, exemplified not only by "La Pierre qui pousse" and "Les Muets" but also, somewhat more obscurely and obliquely, by the piece called "L'Hote"—the type, that is, which speaks of the human communion itself as the power by which man can alone hope to prevail and to endure beyond the time when, as William Faulkner says, "the last dingdong of doom has clanged and faded from the last worthless rock hanging tideless in the last red and dying evening." The three other stories in the volume—"La Femme Adultère," "Le Renégat," and "Jonas"—are reminiscent in their imagery of the loneliness and abandonment and travail of Camus' earlier doctrine of the Absurd. Written late in his life, they may serve to remind us that, for all his piety towards *l'humaine présence* and *solidarité*, he remained a poet of dereliction and a philosopher of *rébellion*.

IX

Apart from André Malraux and possibly Jean-Paul
Sartre, Camus seemed more ready for dialogue
with the Christian community than any other
French writer of our day who stands outside Christian perspectives. And this was so because, perhaps
beyond all his major contemporaries, Camus, both
as artist and philosopher, canvassed the human
problem with a singular attentiveness to what is
implied for it by the modern crisis of faith. He had,
to be sure, in the course of his meditations discovered that, even in the midst of winter, there
was in himself an invincible summer. And those
of his Christian critics who want to go in for the
closest kind of bargaining have, therefore, been
quick to conclude that his was a position outside
the realm of grace. But I wonder to what extent
it was not rather, in very large part, merely
outside what Dietrich Bonhoeffer liked to call
"cheap grace"—that is, grace as related to a
spatialized and objectified God, understood in
terms of the old metaphysic of transcendence,
or simply as bourgeois respectability without discipleship.[1]

It is true, of course, that Camus for all his
affinity with modern Existentialism (with which his
quarrels were always family quarrels), lived very
much in the universe of classical Stoicism and of
the neo-Stoicism which has been so powerfully

[1] *Vide* Dietrich Bonhoeffer, *The Cost of Discipleship*, trans. by
R. H. Fuller (New York: Macmillan Co., 1949), Chapter I.

expressed in our own period by such writers, super-ficially so different, as Conrad and Hemingway and Faulkner and Malraux. His was not, to be sure, the metaphysic that generally prevailed in ancient Stoicism, for he could not be as certain of the rationality of the world-process as an Epictetus or a Marcus Aurelius, and he remained unconvinced that human life is steadied and protected by any-thing transcendent to itself. But the indifference, the austerity, the *apatheia*, with which Camus' rebel faces the silence of the universe is a Stoic *apatheia*, a Stoic courage: it is, as it was for Seneca, a way of safeguarding what is right and reasonable in the human soul against everything in existence by which it might be mutilated or undone. The rebel, as Camus said, "opposes the principle of justice which he finds in himself to the principle of in-justice which he sees being applied in the world."

Yet, despite the heavily Stoical cast of Camus' mind, there is one very important respect in which his moral and religious vision is profoundly differ-ent from that of classical Stoicism. And it is a differ-ence of which we may be put in mind by an observation which Paul Tillich makes of the Stoics: he says:

The Stoic as a Stoic does not experience the despair of personal guilt. Epictetus quotes as an example Socrates' words in Xenophon's *Memora-bilia*: "I have maintained that which is under my control" and "I have never done anything that was wrong in my private or in my public life." And Epictetus himself asserts that he has learned not to care for anything that is outside the realm of his moral purpose. But more revealing than such statements is the general attitude of superiority and complacency which characterizes the Stoic *diatribai*, their moral orations and public accusations. The Stoic cannot say, as Hamlet does, that "conscience" makes cowards of us *all*. He does not see the universal fall from essential rationality to existential foolishness as a matter of responsibility and as a problem of guilt. The courage to be for him is the courage to affirm oneself in spite of fate and death, but it is not the courage to affirm oneself in spite of sin and guilt.[1]

For Camus, however, we are all, as Tarrou says, *dans la peste*, and nowhere in recent literature can we find a more trenchant analysis of the depth of the moral problem than in the closing pages of *L'Homme révolté*. Here he evinces a profound awareness of how deeply every life is involved in a violation of the law of love and of how tragically contaminated is every expedient man uses to secure a tolerable justice. The rebel wants "to serve justice so as not to add to the injustice of the human condition": so "he cannot turn away from the world and from history without denying the very principle of his rebellion." Yet to involve oneself in the drama of history is to be overtaken by the uneasiness of conscience that results from our discovery of the moral ambiguity inherent in every choice, in every option: there is no "motive that does not have its limits in evil." To renounce the project of making the human person respected is to "renounce rebellion and fall back on an attitude of nihilistic consent." Yet to "insist that human identity should be

[1] Paul Tillich, *op. cit.*, p. 17.

recognized as existing" is to undertake a commitment that will prevent my unqualified rejection of violence. "If the rebel makes no choice, he chooses the silence and slavery of others. If, in a moment of despair, he declares that he opts both against God and against history, he is the witness of pure freedom; in other words, of nothing." But, then, to ally oneself with the struggle *for* man is to pledge oneself to an effort that may in some sense entail a vindication of murder—despite the fact that "rebellion, in principle, is a protest against death." Thus, as Camus says in the passage from which I have already quoted, "the rebel can never find peace. He knows what is good and, despite himself, does evil." "Rebellion . . . sets us on the path of calculated culpability," and it is in *la mésure* that we have the one hope of its being redeemed.

So, though in some measure the vision of this Frenchman has its affiliation with the Stoic tradition, he clearly in no wise represents the moral complacency of classical Stoicism. On the contrary: he tells us that the rebel must face the moral ambiguity of human existence "indefatigably." And the question, therefore, arises as to how, within the perspectives of Camus' thought, this is possible. What was it, in other words, that enabled him to affirm the human enterprise as passionately as he did, "in spite of sin and guilt"?

The answer to this question is, I believe, to be found in its clearest form in his early book *Noces* (published in Algiers by Charlot in 1938), in the volume of essays called *L'Eté* (published in Paris by Gallimard in 1954), and in the final chapter of *L'Homme révolté*. We are reminded, when we turn to the book of 1938, that Camus, having grown up in Algeria, was by birth and nurture a North African, and the four essays that comprise this slender volume are devoted to the Mediterranean countryside which formed the scene of his youth. They are a veritable "manual of happiness," and what is celebrated is a "loving alliance" between man and the earth—the riot and play and fecundity, the glory and the grandeur of the world. Camus speaks of places, of Tipasa and Djémila and Algiers and Florence: he speaks of the heat of the sun, of the magnificence of the sea, of the tanned bodies on the beach, of the cool evenings and the quiet Mediterranean dusks. He makes us smell the heavy fragrances of North African plants: he makes us see the riotous colours of the Tuscan landscape: and we are drenched in the rich, sensual carnality of wind and rain, of gardens and the desert, of sky and sea. He records how, as a youth, he "learned to consent to the earth and to burn in the dark flame of its celebrations." And, in one characteristic sentence, he says: "I must be naked and plunge into the sea ... and consummate on my own flesh the embrace for which, lips to lips, earth and sea have for so long been sighing."

The message, in other words, of *Noces* is that "if there is a sin against life, it is perhaps not so much in despairing as in hoping for another life, and in concealing the implacable grandeur of this one." And thus the author of this book was bent on surrendering himself utterly to "the happy lassitude of my nuptials with the world." In what is perhaps the key essay in the volume, the opening essay which is called "Noces à Tipasa," he records how, on one gloriously beautiful spring day, amidst, the melodious sighings of the Algerian countryside, he opened his "eyes and heart to the intolerable grandeur of that sky gorged with heat." And it is a similarly "lucid attention" before the great enchantments of the earth which is called for in the other meditations—"Le Vent à Djémila," "L'Eté à Alger," and "Le Désert"—which comprise this beautiful and moving little book.

It is this same opulence of language, of emotion, of love, that animates the essays written between 1939 and 1953 which were brought together in *L'Eté*. In *Noces* Camus was attempting to express the "simple accord" that he felt between himself and the rich, luxuriant field of life, and it is this same purpose which controls the rhetoric of the eight meditations that form *L'Eté*. "In the centre of our work," he says in this book, "shines an inexhaustible sun," and it is this—the dazzling brilliance and beauty and splendour of the world—it is this, he confesses, that protects him against despair. And in the essay called "Retour à Tipasa," there occurs a crucial passage in which he says:

At noon on the half-sandy slopes covered with heliotropes like a foam left by the furious waves of the last few days as they withdrew, I watched the sea barely swelling at that hour with an exhausted motion, and I satisfied the two thirsts one cannot long neglect without drying up—I mean loving and admiring. For there is merely bad luck in not being loved; there is misfortune in not loving. All of us, today, are dying of this misfortune. For violence and hatred dry up the heart itself; the long fight for justice exhausts the love that nevertheless gave birth to it. . . . But in order to keep justice from shrivelling up like a beautiful orange fruit containing nothing but a bitter, dry pulp, I discovered once more at Tipasa that one must keep intact in oneself a freshness, a cool wellspring of joy, love the day that escapes injustice, and return to combat having won that light. . . . In the middle of winter I at last discovered that there was in me an invincible summer.

Now this "invincible summer" is not any mere Stoic *apatheia*, it is no mere capacity for endurance, for martial fortitude, for preserving the stiff lip despite the assaults of experience: it is, instead, something glowing and positive and does, indeed, I believe, partake of what Paul Tillich, with his genius for definition, has called "absolute faith," the faith which creates the courage of self-affirmation not only "in spite of fate and death" but also "in spite of sin and guilt."

An analysis of the nature of absolute faith [says Dr. Tillich] reveals the following elements in it. The first is the experience of the power of being which is present even in face of the most radical manifestation of nonbeing. . . . The vitality that can stand the abyss of meaninglessness is aware of a hidden meaning within the destruction of meaning. The second element in absolute faith is the dependence of the experience of nonbeing on the experience of being and the dependence of the experience of meaninglessness on the experience of meaning. Even in the state of despair one has enough being to make despair possible. There is a third element in absolute faith, the acceptance of being accepted. Of course, in the state of despair there is nobody and nothing that accepts. But there is the power of acceptance itself which is experienced. Meaninglessness, as long as it is experienced, includes an experience of the "power of acceptance." To accept this power of acceptance consciously is the religious answer of absolute faith, of a faith which has been deprived by doubt of any concrete content, which nevertheless is faith and the source of the most paradoxical manifestation of the courage to be.[1]

This analysis seems very nearly to describe Camus' affirming vision of life. Was not the invincible summer that he discovered in the midst of winter his testimony to an "experience of the power of being . . . in face of the most radical manifestation of nonbeing"? And were not the hymns in *Noces* and *L'Eté* to the beautiful plenitude and splendour of the world his testimony to an experience of being at one with Being-itself, an experience that went deeper even than the experience of the Absurd? He speaks in *Noces* of "the smile of complicity" that he "exchanged" with the brilliant smile of the Mediterranean sea and sky and wind and stars, and I wonder if this may not have been his obscure testimony to a deep intuition of something like what Dr. Tillich calls "the power of acceptance." Perhaps this was what *enabled* him to bear the knowledge that, though the rebel is not ignorant of what is good, nevertheless, he does evil. Rebellion, he says in the final chapter of *L'Homme révolté*, "cannot exist without a strange form of love"—the love, that is, of "the real grandeur" of the world; and it

[1] Paul Tillich, *op. cit.*, p. 177.

is out of this love that there is born "that strange joy which helps one to live and die."

It may be, in other words, that Camus really did know something that approximates the Christian experience of justification, and that perhaps in some sense he did really apprehend "the God above the God of theism." It is true, of course, that in him a very radical scepticism had undercut most of the concrete symbolism of Christian faith, and a profound impatience with conventional religious apologetics inhibited any decisive movement in the direction of the metaphysical personalism of biblical faith. But surely it is clear that in Camus there was an equally profound sense of the "transpersonal presence of the divine"[1] which is also an element of biblical faith; and we have, I think, ample testimony in his writings that this was for him a rich and deep source of the confidence and the courage that enabled him to go "beyond nihilism." So perhaps this was a modern man who did not altogether live outside the realm of grace.

Camus was in mid-career at the time of his death; and it is said that there was then a vast novel in progress that was to be called *Le premier homme*, and also a long essay to be called "Le Mythe de Némésis"; and there are still other rumours of additional works that were at various stages of accomplishment on his desk. Whatever final definition we may attempt of his work and his testimony, it will not be that at which he aimed and must forever remain incomplete. Certainly, it would be wrong to suggest any kind of posthumous baptism; yet it is surely an equally wrong reading of his story of our time, even as far as he was able to develop it, to

[1] Paul Tillich, *op. cit.*, p. 187.

argue that it contains no more than the "neo-paganism" or "existentialist nihilism," of so much conventional criticism.

In an eloquent statement in *The Atlantic Monthly* in the spring of 1958, Charles Rolo spoke of Camus as "a good man,"[1] and, though I suspect that he may himself have been embarrassed when his critics responded to him as though he were "a moral force," it is, nevertheless, something of the sort that we feel. For here was a man who in no way chose to live at any comfortable remove from the tension and unrest of his age. As participant in the French Resistance during the war years, as newspaper editor and political ideologist, as theatrical director in the Parisian theatre, as artist and thinker, he lived at the very centre of the maelstrom of contemporary history, and he did this without recourse to any of the false safeties and securities by which European intellectuals in this century have sometimes been compromised: he did this only with the courage of a kind of "absolute faith" which passionately affirmed the worth of the human enterprise in spite of its apparent "absurdity." And through him we have a noble example of "the courage to be" in a representative man of our age—rooted, perhaps, "in the God who appears when God has disappeared in the anxiety of doubt."[2] The Swedish Academy was, I believe, right when, in the Nobel Prize citation of 1957, it honoured him for illuminating "the problems of the human conscience in our time." This was the remarkable feat that this distinguished young writer had achieved,

---

[1] Charles Rolo, "Albert Camus: A Good Man," *The Atlantic Monthly*, Vol. 201, No. 5 (May, 1958).

[2] Paul Tillich, *op. cit.*, p. 190.

and it is to be hoped that those whose confessions of faith are fuller and more robust than his will not forgo the risks of joining with him in the kind of dialogue which all of his work, in the most vital way, implicitly proposes.

On the seventh day of November, 1913, Albert
Camus was born in the little Algerian village of
Mondovi, "on the shores of a happy sea." His
mother was Spanish, and his father was a Frenchman of Alsatian background who was killed in the
Battle of the Marne only a few months after
Albert's birth. Throughout Camus' childhood the
family was in desperately straitened financial circumstances and lived on the closest kind of eco-
nomic margin, his mother being able, as a char-
woman, to earn only the most meagre living for
Albert and his brother in Algiers, to which she and
her sons moved following her husband's death.
Their residence was in the working-class district of
Belcourt, and it was here that Camus received his
early education in the state schools.

It was in 1923 that one of his teachers, Louis Ger-
main, helped him to win a scholarship to the *lycée*
in Algiers, and here he pursued the studies that prepared him to enter the University of Algiers in
1932. His university course was in philosophy, and
it culminated in 1936 in a thesis on the relations between Augustine and Neo-Platonism. But, as a
university student in the 'thirties, Camus was not
only reading classical Greek and German philosophy and such modern thinkers as Heidegger and
Jaspers and Shestov: he was also deeply immersed
in modern French literature, and it was doubtless
his tutelage under writers like Proust and Gide and
Montherlant and Malraux that gave birth to his

desire for a literary career. Throughout this period, in addition to his literary and intellectual interests (in which his great guide was Jean Grenier, a professor in the University of Algiers), his enormous enthusiasm for sport—particularly swimming— was unremitting, despite the occasional flare-ups of a tubercular condition which was first detected in 1930.

Like so many other young men of his generation, Camus found the attitude of neutrality impossible with respect to the important issues of domestic and international politics in the 'thirties, and, in 1934, he joined the Communist Party, thus undertaking the particular allegiance whose vogue among intellectuals was then world-wide. He remained a Communist, however, only for a few months, soon leaving the Party in disgust with the capricious and unjustified changes in its strategy in relation to the Moslem population in Algeria. But, though he quickly lost all patience with the dogmatic cabalism of the Communist movement, in one particular he was deeply affected by the cultural atmosphere that Marxism helped to promote in the nineteen-thirties —and this concerned the new connection that was everywhere envisaged between the arts and the life of the working classes. It was largely as a result of his involvement in this aspect of Communism that he devoted himself to the establishment of a workers' theatre in Algiers, which came into being in 1935 as "Le Théâtre du travail." In a few months it had, under slightly modified ideological auspices, become "Le Théâtre de l'équipe," but not before Camus had shared with some of his associates in the "collective" experiment of jointly writing with them, and producing, a play on the revolt of the

miners in Oviedo in 1934 (*Révolte dans les Asturies*).
For the next two or three years, with Camus as the
central figure, this group produced numerous
adaptations of novels and plays from both classical
and modern literatures.

As the 'thirties drew to a close, Camus was not
only deeply engaged in *avant-garde* theatrical enterprise, but he was also a busy reporter and editorial
writer on the staff of Pascal Pia's *Alger-Républicain*:
his philosophic and literary studies went on un-
abated, and his creative work had already begun,
L'Envers et l'endroit having appeared in 1937, *Noces*
in 1938 and *Caligula* being written in the same year
(though its publication was to be delayed until
1944). But, with the outbreak of international war
in the fateful month of September, 1939, writing
and creative labour in the theatre and travel were
for a time all brought to a halt, and Camus immediately volunteered for military duty. The frailty
of his physical constitution, however, made his rejection inevitable, and, after spending several
months in a futile effort to secure some sort of
government post that would be useful in the crisis,
he went to Paris in March of 1940, there to join the
staff of the evening paper *Paris-Soir*. But then came
the German invasion in May, and the subsequent
Occupation meant, of course, the end of a free press
in France. So, after a few months amidst the dreari-
ness of Lyons, where he completed *Le Mythe de
Sisyphe*, Camus returned to Algeria in January of
1941, and it was there that he began to plot the work
which was to be published six years later as *La Peste*.

By 1942 the Resistance movement was well under
way, and so Camus joined the network whose
headquarters were in Lyons and which called itself

Combat. After a time his chief assignment with this group came to be an editorial job on the staff of the network's paper which bore the organization's name; and it was through his work for *Combat* that he was brought into close association with André Malraux, whom for so many years he had admired, and the poet René Leynaud, who was executed by the Germans in the spring of 1944. *Combat* quickly became one of the leading newspapers in France after the liberation of Paris in August of 1944, and for the next three years its distinguished editor was Albert Camus, the brilliant young writer whom the French public was coming to know as the author of the remarkable first novel, *L'Etranger*, which Gallimard had published in 1942, and as the author of *Le Malentendu* (first presented at the Théâtre des Mathurins in 1944) and *Caligula*, which caused a sensation when it was first presented at the Théâtre-Hébertot in Paris in 1945.

By 1947 the author of *Le Mythe de Sisyphe* and *La Peste* was a famous and celebrated presence in French literary and intellectual life. And in '47, after numerous policy disagreements with his *Combat* colleagues, Camus resigned his editorial post, having presented to France in the years immediately following the Liberation the example of a brilliant journalism unswerving in its dedication to a radically leftist position unaffiliated with the Communist Party.

After his resignation from *Combat* Camus withdrew from public life, and there followed a period of intense creativity which saw the brilliant first productions of *L'Etat de siège* at the Théâtre Marigny in Paris in October of '48 and *Les Justes* at the Hébertot in December of '49, the appearance of his first collection of political criticism (*Actuelles I*) in 1950, and, in 1951, the publication of *L'Homme révolté*. The book on rebellion caused a commotion the fierceness of which was spectacular even on the French scene, where the intellectual life is normally an affair of spleen and passion, and it signalized a completion of the rupture that had long been in the making between Camus and Jean-Paul Sartre. The explosion was touched off by one of Sartre's disciples, Francis Jeanson, who published in the May, 1952 number of *Les Temps modernes* a long review of *L'Homme révolté* the gist of which involved the claim that Camus' evasion of history and his preoccupation with "transcendental principles" had rendered him irrelevant to the vicissitudes and distempers of the time. To this attack Camus immediately replied with a long letter to Sartre, the editor of the journal, which Sartre published in his August–September issue, along with his own rebuttal. The crux of Camus' reply was the charge that *Les Temps modernes*, whether wittingly or unwittingly, was pursuing an essentially Stalinist line, in so far as it dismissed as reactionary all criticism of the Marxist movement and claimed Communist inspiration for every revolutionary insurgency. It was indeed entangled, he argued, in the most ironical contradictions, for, whereas its Existentialist orientation committed it to a programme of absolute freedom for man, its Stalinism committed it, ultimately, to a programme of concentration camps and enslavement. "To free man of every restraint only to trap him subsequently in 'historical necessity' amounts," he said, "to depriving him of his reasons for struggling for freedom and leaving him to the mercies of any political party operating by the rules of expediency. This means proceeding, according to the law of nihilism, from absolute freedom to extreme necessity; it implies nothing else but dedication to the enslavement of man." Sartre's reply was to the effect that Camus was a reactionary bourgeois whose moral purism was irrelevant to the actual ambiguities of political existence. Thus the issues were joined, and the debate that ensued was one of the major events in French intellectual life in the early 'fifties.

From 1953 on Camus was once more deeply immersed in theatrical activity, producing in that year stage adaptations of Calderón's *La devoción de la Cruz* and Larivey's *Les Esprits*; of Buzzati's *Un caso clinico* (*Un cas intéressant*) in 1955; of Faulkner's *Requiem for a Nun* (*Requiem pour une nonne*) in 1956; of Lope de Vega's *El caballero de Olmedo* (*Le Chevalier d'Olmédo*) in 1957; and of Dostoievski's *The Possessed* (*Les Possédés*) in 1959. In the second (1953) and third (1958) volumes of *Actuelles* he continued to publish political criticism; and in the volume of 1954 called *L'Eté* he brought together a number of essays whose tone and emphasis harked back to the early lyrical pieces in *Noces*. His novel *La Chute* appeared in 1956, and the collection of stories, *L'Exil et le royaume*, in 1957. And, in addition to his involvement in all his various literary projects, he worked throughout these years as an editor for the publishing house of Gallimard.

His election by the Swedish Academy in 1957, at the age of forty-four, to the high eminence of the Nobel Prize came as a great shock to him, and, on being notified of the Academy's action, his first exclamation was: "Had I been on the Swedish jury, I would have voted for Malraux." In his acceptance speech in Stockholm he chose to speak of the idea by which he had been comforted and sustained throughout his life, even in the most difficult and trying circumstances, the idea of his art and of the writer's vocation. "To me," he said, "art is not a solitary delight. It is a means of stirring the greatest number of men by providing them with a privileged image of our common joys and woes." And so he declared his conviction that the artist "by definition . . . cannot serve today those who make history; he must serve those who are subject to it. Otherwise he is alone and deprived of his art. All the armies of tyranny with their millions of men cannot people his solitude—even, and especially, if he is willing to fall into step with them. But the silence of an unknown prisoner subjected to humiliations at the other end of the world is enough to tear the writer from exile, at least whenever he manages, amid the privileges of freedom, not to forget that silence but to give it voice by means of art."

And here indeed, we feel, was an artist who had found his voice. So it was with the profoundest sorrow that men and women all over the world learned on the fourth of January, 1960, that, early that day, Camus had been killed, when the car in which he was riding with his publisher Michel Gallimard struck a tree near Sens, about seventy-five miles south-east of Paris: not only France but the whole civilized world felt diminished. For everyone had known that, in the little village of Lourmarin at the foot of the Alps, where he now lies buried and where he spent his last years, one of the great spokesmen for the human spirit in this century was in the midst of a career than which there was none more promising in our time.

A SELECTED BIBLIOGRAPHY

I. WORKS BY CAMUS

Fiction

L'Etranger. Paris: Gallimard, 1942. (*The Outsider.* Trans. by Stuart Gilbert. London: Hamish Hamilton, 1946.)

La Peste. Paris: Gallimard, 1947. (*The Plague.* Trans. by Stuart Gilbert. London: Hamish Hamilton, 1948.)

La Chute. Paris: Gallimard, 1956. (*The Fall.* Trans. by Justin O'Brien. London: Hamish Hamilton, 1957.)

L'Exil et le royaume. Paris: Gallimard, 1957. (*Exile and the Kingdom.* Trans. by Justin O'Brien. London: Hamish Hamilton, 1958.)

Drama

A. Original Works

La Révolte dans les Asturies. Algiers: Charlot, 1936.

Le Malentendu, suivi de Caligula. Paris: Gallimard, 1944. (*Caligula and Cross Purpose.* Trans. by Stuart Gilbert. Preface by Camus, translated by Justin O'Brien. London: Hamish Hamilton, 1948.)

L'Etat de siège. Paris: Gallimard, 1948. (*Caligula and Three Other Plays.* Trans. by Stuart Gilbert. New York: Alfred A. Knopf, 1958.)

Les Justes. Paris: Gallimard, 1950. (*Caligula and Three Other Plays.* Trans. by Stuart Gilbert. New York: Alfred A. Knopf, 1958).

B. Translations and Adaptations

Calderón, *La Dévotion à la croix* (*La devoción de la Cruz*). Paris: Gallimard, 1953.

Pierre de Larivey, *Les Esprits*. Paris: Gallimard, 1953.

Dino Buzzati, *Un Cas intéressant* (*Un caso clinico*). Paris: L'Avant-scène, 1955.

Lope de Vega, *Le Chevalier d'Olmédo* (*El caballero de Olmedo*). Paris: Gallimard, 1957.

William Faulkner, *Requiem pour une nonne* (*Requiem for a Nun*). Paris: Gallimard, 1957.

Fyodor Dostoievski, *Les Possédés*. Paris: Gallimard, 1959. (*The Possessed*. Trans. by Justin O'Brien. New York: Alfred A. Knopf, 1960.)

Essays

L'Envers et l'endroit. Algiers: Charlot, 1937. Nouv. éd.: Paris: Gallimard, 1958.

Noces. Algiers: Charlot, 1938. Nouv. éd.: Paris: Gallimard, 1947.

Le Mythe de Sisyphe. Paris: Gallimard, 1942. (*The Myth of Sisyphus*. Trans. by Justin O'Brien. London: Hamish Hamilton, 1955.)

Lettres à un ami allemand. Paris: Gallimard, 1945. (Trans. by Justin O'Brien in *Resistance, Rebellion, and Death*. New York: Alfred A. Knopf, 1961.)

Actuelles: Chroniques, 1944–1948. Paris: Gallimard, 1950.

L'Homme révolté. Paris: Gallimard, 1951. (*The Rebel*. Trans. by Anthony Bower; preface by Sir Herbert Read. London: Hamish Hamilton, 1953.)

Actuelles: Chroniques, 1948–1953. Paris: Gallimard, 1953.

L'Eté. Paris: Gallimard, 1954.

Actuelles: Chronique algérienne, 1939–1958. Paris: Gallimard, 1958.

Discours de Suède. Paris: Gallimard, 1958. (*Speech of Acceptance upon the Award of the Nobel Prize for Literature*. Trans. by Justin O'Brien. New York: Alfred A. Knopf, 1958.)

Resistance, Rebellion, and Death. (Selections from the three volumes of *Actuelles*, together with Camus' essay, "Reflexions sur la guillotine" ("Reflections on the Guillotine"), which originally appeared in the symposium (*Réflexions sur la peine capitale*, Paris: Calmann-Lévy, 1957) on which he collaborated with Arthur Koestler.) Trans. by Justin O'Brien. New York: Alfred A. Knopf, 1961.

II. CRITICAL ASSESSMENTS OF CAMUS' WORK

Georges Bataille, "La temps de la révolte," *Critique*, Nos. 55 and 56 (December 1951 and January 1952), pp. 1019–1027 and pp. 1029–1041.

Rachel Bespaloff, "Le monde du condamné à mort," *Esprit*, Vol. XVIII (January, 1950), pp. 1–26.

Renate Bollinger, *Albert Camus: Eine Bibliographie der Literatur über ihn und sein Werk*. Cologne: Greyen Verlag, 1957. (A most useful check-list that comprehensively canvasses the literature of its subject up to the time of its publication.)

Germaine Brée, *Camus*. New Brunswick: Rutgers University Press, 1961. (A comprehensive evaluation, with excellent bibliographies.)

Jean-Claude Brisville, *Camus*. Paris: Gallimard, 1959.

Robert Champigny, *Sur un héros païen*. Paris: Gallimard, 1959.

Nicola Chiaromonte, "Sartre versus Camus: A Political Quarrel," *Partisan Review*, Vol. XIX, No. 6 (November–December, 1952), pp. 680–686.

John Cruickshank, *Albert Camus and the Literature of Revolt*. London and New York: Oxford University Press, 1959.

Thomas Hanna, *The Thought and Art of Albert Camus*. Chicago: Henry Regnery Co., 1958.

Kermit Lansner, "Albert Camus," *The Kenyon Review*, Vol. XIV, No. 4 (Autumn, 1952), pp. 562–578.

Robert de Luppé, *Albert Camus*. Paris: Editions Universitaires, 1958.

Rogert Quilliot, *La Mer et les prisons: Essai sur Albert Camus*. Paris: Gallimard, 1956. (Contains an excellent checklist of Camus' writings.)

Charles Rolo, "Albert Camus: A Good Man," *The Atlantic Monthly*, Vol. 201, No. 5 (May 1958), pp. 27–33.

Jean-Paul Sartre, "Explication de 'L'Etranger'," *Situations I*. Paris: Gallimard, 1947. (Pp. 99–121.) (Reprinted in Sartre's *Literary and Philosophical Essays*. Trans. by Annette Michelson. London: Rider and Co., 1955.)

Nathan A. Scott, "The Modest Optimism of Albert Camus," *The Christian Scholar*, Vol. XLII, No. 4 (December 1959), pp. 251–274.

Albert Sonnenfeld, "Albert Camus as Dramatist: The Sources of His Failure," *The Tulane Drama Review*, Vol. V, No. 4 (June 1961), pp. 106–123.

Gerald Stourzh, "The Unforgivable Sin: An Interpretation of *The Fall,*" *Chicago Review*, Vol. XV, No. 1 (Summer 1961), pp. 45–57.

Philip Thody, *Albert Camus: A Study of His Work*. London: Hamish Hamilton, 1957.

III. CRITICAL VOLUMES PARTIALLY DEVOTED TO CAMUS

Maurice Blanchot, *Faux pas*. Paris: Gallimard, 1943.

Germaine Brée and Margaret Guiton, *An Age of Fiction: The French Novel from Gide to Camus*. New Brunswick: Rutgers University Press, 1957.

Pierre Brodin, *Présences contemporaines*, Vol. I. Paris: Nouvelles éditions Debresse, 1956.

Anthony Curtis, *New Developments in the French Theatre*. London: The Curtain Press, 1948.

Wallace Fowlie, *A Guide to Contemporary French Literature*. New York: Meridian Books, 1957.

Wallace Fowlie, *Dionysus in Paris: A Guide to Contemporary French Theatre*. New York: Meridian Books, 1960.

R. W. B. Lewis, *The Picaresque Saint: Representative Figures in Contemporary Fiction*. Philadelphia and New York: J. B. Lippincott Co., 1959.

René Marill, *La révolte des écrivains d'aujourd'hui*. Paris: Correa, 1949.

Claude Mauriac, *Hommes et idées d'aujourd'hui*. Paris: Albin Michel, 1953.

Claude Mauriac, *La littérature contemporaine*. Paris: Albin Michel, 1958.

Charles Moeller, *Littérature du XXe siècle et christianisme*, Vol. I (*Silence de Dieu*). Paris: Casterman, 1953.

Emmanuel Mounier, *L'Espoir des désespérés*. Paris: Seuil, 1953.

William R. Mueller, *The Prophetic Voice in Modern Fiction*. New York: Association Press, 1959.

Henri Peyre, *The Contemporary French Novel*. New York: Oxford University Press, 1955.